The
PHYSICIAN
ASSISTANT
in a Changing
Health Care Environment

Gretchen Engle Schafft, Ph.D., M.H.S.
Senior Project Director
COSMOS Corporation
Washington, D.C.

James F. Cawley, M.P.H., P.A.-C.
Associate Professor of Health Care Science
Physician Assistant Program
George Washington University Medical Center
Washington, D.C.

AN ASPEN PUBLICATION
Aspen Publishers, Inc.
Rockville, Maryland
Royal Tunbridge Wells
1987

Library of Congress Cataloging-in-Publication Data

Schafft, Gretchen E.
The physician assistant in a changing health
care environment.

"An Aspen publication."
Includes bibliographies and index.
1. Physicians' assistants—United States.
2. Medical care—United States. I. Cawley, James F.
II. Title [DNLM 1. Physicians' Assistants.
W21.5 S296p]
R697.P45S33 1987   610.69'53   87-17450
ISBN: 0-87189-870-5

Editorial Services: Carolyn Ormes

Library of Congress Catalog Card Number: 87-17450
ISBN: 0-87189-870-5

Printed in the United States of America

1 2 3 4 5

For
Otto and Erika Roth
and
Roberta Hall Cawley

Contents

Foreword ix
  Henry J. Aaron

Preface xi

Acknowledgments xiii

Chapter 1—The Development of a Profession in a Shifting
           Ideological Climate 1
      Birth of the Physician Assistant Profession 2
      Educational Training Programs 5
      Quality of Care Provided by the Physician Assistant 9
      Current Characteristics of the Profession 10
      Cost-Containment Emphasis in Health Care 10

Chapter 2—Negotiated Roles and Alliances 21
      Negotiated Roles and Alliances 24
      Nonnegotiable Aspects of the Role 25
      Credentialing of Physician Assistants 29
      Refining the Definition of Physician Assistant 33
      Prescribing Rights of Physician Assistants 35
      Meaning of Dependent Practice and Supervision 36
      Role Negotiation for the Physician Assistant 38
      Emerging Roles for Physician Assistants 41
      Conclusion 41

Chapter 3—Provision of Care to the Underserved: The Physician Assistant's Role **45**
   The Physician Assistant's Role 48
   Early Concern for the Underserved 48
   Indications of Increased Access to Care 49
   Continuing Problems in Receiving Medical Care 50
   Those Most at Risk 52
   Minority Representation in the Physician Assistant
      Profession 55
   Conclusion 61

Chapter 4—The Cost Effectiveness of Physician Assistants **65**
   The Cost Effectiveness of Physician Assistants 68
   Limitations of Cost-Effectiveness Analysis 69
   Review of the Literature 70
   From the Data to the Real World 72
   Conclusion 84

Chapter 5—The Physician Assistant and Public Health Issues **89**
   The Physician Assistant and Public Health Issues 92
   History of the Public Health Field 92
   Technological Advances and Public Health 94
   New Diseases and Menaces 96
   Health Promotion and Disease Prevention 103
   Conclusion 106

Chapter 6—The Physician Assistant in Hospitals **109**
   The Physician Assistant in Hospitals 111
   Extent of Utilization 111
   Inpatient Roles and Functions 113
   Privileges, Supervision, and Credentialing 119
   Costs, Reimbursement, and DRGs 126
   Conclusion 127

Chapter 7—Physician Assistants in the Medical Marketplace **131**
   Physician Assistants in the Medical Marketplace 134
   Assumptions of the Marketplace 134
   Characteristics of the Competitive Environment 136
   Corporate Structure and Managed Care 138
   Government Regulation 139
   Health Care Organizations in the Competitive Model 143
   What the New Trends Mean to the Physician Assistant ... 147

Chapter 8—Geriatric Care and the Physician Assistant **153**
    Geriatric Care and the Physician Assistant 156
    A New Era of Geriatric Interest 157
    Growth of Geriatric Health Care Costs 159
    Physician Assistants' Involvement in Geriatrics
        Increases 162
    Conclusion 173

Chapter 9—Specialization and Career Mobility **175**
    Specialization and Career Mobility 178
    Original Concept of the Profession 178
    Beginning of Specialization in the Medical Profession 180
    Growing Specialization of Physician Assistants:
        Problem or Opportunity? 181
    Professional Attrition 191
    Military Physician Assistants 192
    Pathways of Career Advancement 194
    Conclusion 196

Chapter 10—Physician Assistants in the Future **199**
    Physician Assistants in the Future 201
    Re-emergence of Equity Issues 201
    Alternative Delivery of Health Care 204
    The Physician Assistant in a Multitiered Health Care
        System 205
    The Future of Dependent Practice 207
    Lessons from Other Systems 208
    Containing the "Oversupply" of Medical Practitioners ... 209
    Continuing Federal Involvement in the Physician
        Assistant Profession 211
    Reassessing the Physician Assistant Movement 214
    Prescription for Continued Growth and Success 214

Index **221**

Foreword

In the late 1960s, the development of a new profession of physician assistants who were capable of performing many of the services normally offered by physicians seemed to offer a kind of deliverance from a multitude of problems. A physician shortage was thought to be imminent. Many neighborhoods or communities already lacked physician services. Furthermore, the spread of third-party coverage was generating a large increase in the demand for health care. Working alone for routine procedures and under a physician's supervision for more sophisticated procedures, physician assistants seemed likely to increase the availability of high-quality care. Because they were paid less than physicians, it was hoped that physician assistants would also reduce costs. The prospects for expansion of the new profession seemed highly favorable, provided that state and federal regulations did not stifle its growth.

Today, the climate for physician assistants is far more complex. Governments, businesses, and other groups are striving to slow the growth of medical costs. Moreover, there is some doubt that the physician shortage, like the missile gap of a slightly earlier period, ever existed. Even if it did, the anticipatory effort to enlarge the number and size of medical schools has been widely successful and now seems almost certain to lead to a huge physician glut.

Taken in isolation, the replacement of a physician shortage with a physician glut augurs ill for the employment prospects of physician assistants. Other factors are at work, however. Three stand out as critical to the long-term prospects for physician assistants: (1) continuing concerns about the rising costs of medical care, (2) the rapid evolution of medical technology, and (3) the sharp increase in the number of elderly persons.

Efforts to reduce the rate at which medical costs are rising can redound to the benefit of physician assistants, but only if they dispense high-quality medical care at less cost than do physicians and only if insurance and regulatory policies permit them to do so. The effects of the revolution in medical technology on physician assistants are ambiguous; the increasing complexity and scientific sophistication of some new procedures may make it impossible for physician assistants to perform them, but the large number of new procedures that can safely be performed by physician assistants with specialized training may free more intensively trained medical professionals to take advantage of new opportunities to perform time-intensive procedures.

The aging of the population, in the end, may provide the most important opportunities for physician assistants. Although illness at any age can cause a combination of somatic, psychological, and social problems, the elderly are especially prone to illnesses that combine these elements. Traditionally, however, the training of physicians has emphasized the diagnosis and treatment of the somatic aspects of illnesses. Although this emphasis is already undergoing some change and may change further, most physicians for many more years to come will have completed their training before such changes in medical curricula were instituted. Because of the shorter training period for physician assistants, geriatric curricula may affect their practice more immediately.

Physician assistants may have more time than do medical doctors to devote to the multifaceted problems of the elderly. To deal with these problems effectively, physician assistants will have to combine the skills in treating somatic aspects of illness that are the core of their original training with broad-based functions that place them squarely within the health care team. In short, physician assistants may be able to respond more effectively than physicians can to certain of the problems of the elderly precisely because physician assistants have not had to make as large an investment in the enormously complex range of science within which modern treatment of somatic problems is lodged.

Given the multiple uncertainties facing the new profession of physician assistants, a guide to the development of the profession, its current status, and its future prospects can be extremely valuable to those in the field and to those who formulate medical care policy. The future of the fledgling profession of physician assistants will depend on technological and economic events over which its members have little or no control. It will also depend on policies concerning reimbursement and licensing that are very much under the control of legislators and health care administrators. *The Physician Assistant in a Changing Health Care Environment*, by Gretchen Engle Schafft and James F. Cawley, can enlighten both those who are trying to provide care and those who are setting policies within which these providers must operate.

Henry J. Aaron, Ph.D.
Senior Fellow, Economic Studies Program, Brookings Institution
and
Professor of Economics, University of Maryland

Preface

America is known as an innovative society with a penchant for developing and adapting useful ideas to meet current situations. Less acknowledged is the notion that these ideas usually fit an ideological context that is rooted in the country's basic value structure, but is also time-specific. Our book examines one such innovation, the physician assistant, within the framework of a changing health care environment. Health care planners, who only a few years ago assumed the task of making the American health care system more accessible to the economically and geographically disadvantaged, are now struggling to make the health care system less costly and to place it squarely within a rational economic framework. In this book, we argue that physician assistants will have to continue to prove themselves as providers of accessible *and* cost effective health care. The thesis of the book is that any innovation that will remain viable in this country will have to adapt the operant values, equity and economic efficiency, which are at the opposite ends of the continuum that spans American values from altruism to self interest. In other words, Americans want to be fair and see that everyone has an equal chance, but they also want to support a business ethic, which means managing the production of goods and services in an efficient way to make a profit.

We two authors bring different backgrounds to writing this book. Gretchen Schafft is an anthropologist whose background is in the study of equity issues in both education and health care. She served for several years as the Director of Research for the American Academy of Physician Assistants. James Cawley is a physician assistant who has written about the profession for various audiences and who teaches physician assistant students at the George Washington University Medical Center. Both of us hold degrees from the John Hopkins School of Hygiene and Public Health and share a perspective on the history and delivery of health care in the United States. We are both avid observers of health policy formation.

Our conviction, there is a need for a book that places physician assistants in the midst of health policy debates, came from our involvement with the profession during a time when demands for proof of physician assistant cost-effectiveness seemed pervasive. Congress was considering including physician assistant services under Medicare reimbursement and required more information about the costs and benefits of using physician assistants in various settings. We were both involved in developing the arguments, and noted a need to develop new materials and to document new trends. Early reports on the profession often focused specifically on issues concerning access to care. Existing literature did not address the salient issues directly or provide the information on physician assistants needed to meet the new questions being raised. At the same time, we felt that the physician assistant's role in providing greater access and quality of care needed to be reaffirmed.

This book, then, explores the growth of the physician assistant enterprise from the point of view of the evolving health care environment since 1967. Emphasis is placed on the changing assumptions by the American public and their health planners about where physician assistants fit into the health care system and how they are adapting to the shift in focus from access to care to cost effectiveness.

Physician Assistants in a Changing Health Care Environment is intended for physician assistants, their supervising physicians, their employers, and health policy analysts and researchers. We hope that these and others will find that the information about the development of the profession and its place in the current scene helps them better understand current health care issues and the evolving role of the physician assistant within them. We believe that this book fills a gap in the literature by placing the physician assistant in the center of health care issues of the day.

Gretchen Engle Schafft
James F. Cawley

Acknowledgments

We thank our friends and colleagues within the physician assistant profession and others who contributed to our understanding of the concepts presented here. The American Academy of Physician Assistants under the direction of F. Lynn May provided us access to current data and background information on the profession without which the book could not have been written. We were gratified by the cooperation of those physician assistants whose thoughtful comments are found in interviews at the beginning of the chapters. Lyn J. Madden held early discussions of the book's basic concept and premise when she served as an intern at the American Academy of Physician Assistants. Many of her contributions are found in the first chapter and she gave meaningful support at the beginning of the project. Nicole Gara, Director of Governmental Affairs for the American Academy of Physician Assistants, made substantial suggestions for the chapter on Negotiated Roles and Alliances, and other staff members, notably Elizabeth Sheley, Kate Holbrook, William Fingerfrock, and Natalie Thompson, contributed in various important ways. Patricia DeLoughry initially typed the manuscript, and did more than that: She managed the manuscript files in such a way as to facilitate the entire project. E. Jane Walters and Nancy Barton provided further assistance with typing and made corrections and suggestions as they went through the manuscript.

Paul Lombardo, R. Scott Chavez, and Paul Hendricks reviewed the entire manuscript carefully from the point of view of physician assistants and made useful suggestions for clarification of the issues. Sherrie Borden, Ron Nelson, Glen Combs, and John Ott reviewed sections of the manuscript and provided valuable comments and pointed critique.

Colleagues at the George Washington University Physician Assistant Program, particularly John Ott, Chairman of the Department of Health Care Science, Walter Stein, Director of the program, and Jarrett Wise and Richard K. Riegelman, were most generous in their support of the project.

We are grateful to our teachers and mentors at the John Hopkins School of Hygiene and Public Health, notably Harvey Brenner, Karen Davis, Margaret Dear, Archie S. Golden, David Levine, Laura Morlock, Vincente Navarro, Thomas Simpson, and Edyth Schoenrich, for their guidance and perspectives on health policy. Others among our colleagues who contributed to our understanding of the concepts presented here are Robert Curry, Craig DeAtley, L.M. Detmer, Joyce Emilio, Bruce C. Fichandler, J. Jeffrey Heinrich, Roderick Hooker, Paul Moson, Henry Perry, J.N.P. Struthers, and Shlomo S. Twersky.

Finally, we thank our spouses, Harry Schafft and Suzanne Cawley, and our children for their patience, understanding, and generosity in allowing us the time we needed to complete this manuscript. Their support and interest made the book possible.

Chapter 1

The Development of a Profession in a Shifting Ideological Climate

Cost containment and cost effectiveness are key words in today's health care debate. The tenor of this debate is almost hysterical as the possibility that we shall bankrupt our future with unbridled spending for the nation's health care is argued. Buzz words cut short meaningful discussion on the state of the health care economy. Few laymen understand the meaning of budget crises or their impact on the future care of the medically needy and ill in the country. The public experiences anxiety about the future of services without the benefit of a great deal of information from which to make independent judgments. Such phrases as "the corporatization of health care" and "the coming bankruptcy of the Medicare system" and descriptions of new programs and permutations of existing ones as "revenue neutral" confuse, rather than enlighten.

In the environment of the mid-1980s, concepts of importance in another era are not only passé, but are unwelcome in the discussion of health care. Equity, right to care, access to health care services sound somehow untutored and old-fashioned.

It was only a little more than two decades ago, however, that a different climate of opinion prevailed. Lyndon Johnson went before Congress in 1965 and said[1]:

> Our first concern must be to assure that the advances of medical knowledge leave none behind. We can and we must strive now to assure the availability of and accessibility to the best health care for all Americans, regardless of age or geography or economic status.

How can it be that in a span of 20 years the ideology underlying health care could have made such a radical shift? What does it mean to a profession to be born into one set of expectations and to come to maturity under another? This book examines the physician assistant profession, the influences that were present at its inception, and its responses to current pressures for rejustification of its usefulness in the configuration of American health care.

American values are diverse and often contradictory. Themes emerge, but consensus rarely develops. Such is the plurality of American society.

Two major themes recur, however, in an almost constant contest for center stage in American thought and domestic policy: equality and market freedom.[2,3] These two themes hang in the balance in decisions at all levels of government. At times, equity is the dominant concern and at other times competition and free market forces come to the fore. At no time, however, is either concern completely put aside. They are two polar ends of a diverse range of opinions, and public policy is made by taking both ends into account. It is almost predictable that, if policy leans too far in one direction or the other, public forces will move to rebalance the scales.

In a pluralistic country, such as the United States, policy is created through many different routes and originates in many different groups and segments of society. A policy may originate in the White House or, before an election, in party platforms and speeches of candidates. It can come from committees in Congress or individual Congressmen who deal with the issues current in American life. It can develop in the courts as the issues are arbitrated and clarified in the judicial system. The citizenry as a whole can demand the formation of policy through public outcry and outrage at perceived inequities and social problems. Even individuals can see their own concerns translated into policy through their lobbying efforts.

Different periods in this country's history have been characterized by a movement to one end of the equity/market freedom spectrum or the other. When that happens, innovations are likely to develop that reflect that perspective. So it was in the 1960s, with the development of the physician assistant profession. This innovation was developed as the mood of the country swung to the equity pole with more force than at any time since the New Deal of the 1930s. The new profession arose from a climate of opinion, a feeling of inclusiveness and generosity that coincided with the availability of a source of health manpower unclaimed by any other health profession.

BIRTH OF THE PHYSICIAN ASSISTANT PROFESSION

The physician assistant profession was born in the mid-1960s. As with any health manpower innovation, it could not be inaugurated solely by those who would provide care or those who would train the new providers. It had to become policy through legitimization from the health care establishment, layers of government, educational institutions, and the public. This meant that it had to be born into a strong political base on a foundation of positive public opinion. The ideological basis of the profession was lodged in arguments concerning equity.

In the mid-1960s, access to health care for the old, the poor, and rural and inner city needy was clearly defined as a priority. The country's leadership made it clear that an equitable distribution of health care services could be accomplished. To back this assertion, federal participation in health care increased with a series of initiatives never before witnessed in the United States. Medicare and Medicaid were established as amendments to the Social Security Act in 1965. Direct payments were made to localities to support the concept that, in America, health care would be made available to all.

There was little debate about the place of health care in the range of rights and privileges of citizenship. It was assumed to be a right that had been too long neglected. To expand the rights of health care, the lack of insurance coverage for the poor and the elderly was remedied in the hope that both the quality and quantity of health care services received by them would equal that enjoyed by other segments of the populace.

The demand for health care services brought into focus a debate on the supply of practitioners. It became a widely held belief that there was a shortage of medically trained personnel. This belief originated in the 1959 Report of the Surgeon General's Consultant Group on Medical Education, which outlined the areas where the medical establishment and government perceived an impending short-age in health care provision.[4] This shortage was thought to be specifically in the area of private or primary care physicians. The report pointed out three reasons why expanded health manpower would be needed:

1. rapid population growth projections (which proved to be excessive) with a disproportionate growth in the young and elderly—populations who statis-tically and historically utilize more health care services,
2. an increased per capita use of health facilities linked to "improved living standards, increased urbanization, more education, widespread use of health insurance, and advances in medical knowledge"
3. an increased number of doctors needed for research, specialization, indus-try, administration, etc.

Although the physician rate per 100,000 had remained fairly constant for the 30 years preceding the report and was 141 per 100,000 in 1959, the percentage of physicians serving as primary care or family physicians, even including the new specialties of internal medicine and pediatrics, had decreased. Primary care physicians furthermore decreased in absolute numbers, making the ratio per 100,000 physicians much smaller.

The report also noted that the public had a growing interest in health care matters and was demanding that more physician time be spent with each patient. This and other constraints, such as increased patient demand to take an active role in medical decision-making, indicated that reorganization of service or instituting greater efficiency would not totally solve the projected shortage. More medical school graduates were needed.

Although the Surgeon General's report advocated the immediate growth of medical schools as a solution, it never recommended growth of the allied health professions or their funding as possible solutions. It also did not address those unserved by the system (the elderly, the poor, the rural) who themselves would create such an expansion in the health care field as they became part of the system through the Medicare and Medicaid legislation of the 1960s. By the mid-1960s it was clear that not only was access to health care affected negatively by this lack of supply of medical personnel but it was also further hampered by the maldistribution of physicians. No one knew what the ideal distribution might be, although the *U.S. News and World Report* stated that one doctor for every 500 patients "is widely regarded as desirable."[5]

The Vietnam War was not unrelated to the debate about solving domestic problems. The "War on Poverty" had brought to public awareness the poverty existing within the bounds of the "richest country on earth," and Johnson's "Great Society" promised to bring solutions to that poverty into being. A "guns and butter" philosophy emerged.[6] Vietnam veterans were coming home with a variety of medical and social problems, but also represented a resource, for many of them had acquired significant medical training and experience on the battlefield.

It is not surprising that the idea of physician assistants developed in this atmosphere. The government was willing to support some of the most far-reaching measures yet devised to increase access to health care, the public showed more support for equity propositions than any time in the previous 30 years, and a source of personnel was available to be tapped.

In the early 1960s, Dr. Charles L. Hudson spoke before the American Medical Association about an idea he had for a new health practitioner. At the same time, Dr. Henry Silver and Loretta Ford, R.N., at the University of Colorado, were discussing the development of a midlevel practitioner who would act as a physician extender to bring medical care to underserved areas. The development of a new health provider was a way to solve the physician shortage without waiting 10 years for a new generation of medical students to enter the field.

The first program for physician assistants began at Duke University in 1965 with a handful of ex-Navy corpsmen under the direction of Eugene Stead, M.D.[7] In addition to the nationally recognized problem of health care shortages, Duke had a specific need for personnel in its own medical center. It was believed that the training period for the new professionals could be much shorter than for medical students because of the previous experience that the physician assistant trainees had gained in their military service. Assurance of competence would be further monitored by the close supervisory role that the physician would fill as the graduates entered practice.

Two basic features of the physician assistant profession were thus instituted. One, the training would be relatively brief in comparison with medical school education. Two, the physician assistant would serve in a supervised practice under the direction of the medical doctor. Emphasis was not placed on development of new skills to differentiate the assistant from the doctor, but on the standard medical model. The physician assistant would be trained to take medical histories, elicit symptoms, develop diagnoses, perform medical tests, and take over some patient management tasks. It was understood that referral of complicated cases or procedures would be made to the supervising physician. Although it was expected that the physician assistant would spend more time on patient education and preventive intervention, all of the skills used by the physician assistant would be those of the physician. This program was not based on a nursing model, and tasks would not be performed independent of physician supervision. Physician assistants would fulfill some, but not all, of the physician's duties.

As one might expect from the description of the 1960s, the federal government entered into the development of the new profession almost immediately. The Department of Health, Education, and Welfare (HEW) provided funds to hold conferences at Duke University under the guidance of Martha Ballinger, J.D. and Harvey E. Estes, Jr., M.D., to develop the concept and work toward model legislation governing physician assistant practice in 1969 and 1970. In 1971 the Health Manpower Act was passed, which provided capitated funding to medical schools for the training of medical personnel to solve the problem of undersupply of medical care in American communities. Physician assistant training programs were included in this funding, which resulted, by 1974, in the doubling of the number of existing training sites to more than 50 such sites. Table 1-1 indicates how this money was allocated.

The American Medical Association (AMA) recognized the physician assistant profession in 1971 and began work on national certification and codification of its practice characteristics. National recognition by the parent group did not ensure universal acceptance by the medical community, however. Occasional roadblocks to physician assistant practice continued to be raised by state chapters of the AMA and medical boards in different areas around the country, causing a distinct variation in practice patterns from state to state.

EDUCATIONAL TRAINING PROGRAMS

The pattern of educational programs has remained the same since the early 1970s. Although variations in its historical roots brought some different titles to the profession, such as child health associate or medex, physician assistant became a generic term for graduates from the accredited programs. All of the programs trained health care personnel to serve the medically needy and the geographically isolated. All of them trained their students to provide medical, not nursing, care in a much shorter time than it takes to train a physician.

Table 1-1 History of Funding Grants for Physician Assistant Training Programs

Year	Number of Programs Funded	Amount (Direct/Indirect)	Max/Min Grant	Average Grant
1972	39	$6,090,109	$327,412 / $15,560	$156,157
1973	36	$6,208,999	$713,451 / $15,538	$172,472
1974	39	$8,129,252	$598,868 / $12,695	$208,442
1975	34	$5,994,002	$321,869 / $44,694	$176,294
1976	35	$6,247,203	$432,690 / $26,000	$176,294
1977	39	$8,171,441	$346,504 / $56,489	$209,524
1978	43	$8,685,074	$340,200 / $22,869	$201,978
1979	42	$8,453,666	$437,117 / $37,453	$201,278
1980	42	$8,262,968	$330,253 / $65,292	$196,737
1981	40	$8,019,000	$429,051 / $45,360	$200,475
1982	34	$4,752,000	$385,464 / $ 6,376	$139,765
1983	34	$4,752,000	$259,817 / $22,279	$139,765
1984	33	$4,414,850	$242,549 / $57,241	$133,783
1985	45	$4,442,076	$225,146 / $19,083	$ 98,713

Source: Bureau of Health Professions, USDHHS, Public Health Service, Health Resources and Services Administration.

The educational programs for physician assistants differ at each location, but most entail about 24 months of training. Approximately half of the educational program is devoted to clinical rotations in which students work in medical settings under close supervision by a physician. In 37 programs a baccalaureate degree is awarded if university requirements are met, and in three a masters degree is an option. From 9 to 12 months of coursework includes the study of subjects such as anatomy, biochemistry, physiology, pharmacology, microbiology, psychology, public health, preventive medicine, physical diagnosis, and biomedical ethics.

Upon conclusion of these educational experiences, the physician assistant assumes a practice role in which he or she is able to:

- approach a patient of any age group in any setting to elicit a detailed and accurate history, perform an appropriate physical examination, delineate problems, and record and present patient data
- analyze health status data obtained via interview, examination, and laboratory diagnostic studies and delineate health care problems in consultation with the physician
- formulate, implement, and monitor an individualized treatment and/or management plan for a patient in consultation with the physician

- instruct and counsel patients regarding compliance with the prescribed therapeutic regimen, normal growth and development, family planning, emotional problems of daily living, and health maintenance
- perform routine procedures essential to managing simple conditions produced by infection or trauma, assist in the management of more complex illness and injury, and initiate evaluations and therapeutic procedures in response to life-threatening situations

In 1983 the institutional affiliations of the 53 physician assistant programs was published by the U.S. Bureau of Health Professions. They are summarized in Table 1-2.

From 1974 until the present time, the physician assistant profession has maintained between 50 and 55 training programs. Graduates have added to the pool of practicing physician assistants until it is estimated that there are about 18,000 in the United States in 1986. There have been no studies of attrition from the profession on a national basis. Therefore, estimates of the number of those in clinical practices are not precise.

Financial support for the training programs comes from the institutions themselves, state money, tuition payments, and federal funding as already discussed. More than half of the students in physician assistant training programs receive financial aid. These programs are relatively small, the average having less than 25 students in each graduating class. Instructors include physician assistants, medical doctors, and educators from allied health fields and nonmedical disciplines.[8]

Table 1-2 Organizational Base for Physician Assistant Programs in 1984: Civilian and Military

	Primary Care	Surgeon's Assistant
Allopathic medical school	18	2
Osteopathic medical school	1	
School of allied health of 4-year college	25	
Community college	6	
Hospital-based	3	1
TOTAL	53	3

Source: Reprinted from *Fifth Report to the President and Congress on the Status of Health Personnel in the United States,* pp. 4–13, Department of Health and Human Services, Bureau of Health Professions, March 1986.

The makeup of the student population has changed over the years. Military corpsmen no longer make up a sizable proportion of the student body, and indeed, women have become the majority student group in physician assistant training programs. Although they are still underrepresented among practicing physician assistants, women are rapidly reaching equal numbers with their male counterparts.

Other population shifts reflect the changing recruitment patterns of the profession. Many of the returning veterans entering the early physician assistant programs were black, but as the general population heard about the professional opportunities of this new career, the original pool was diluted and the black population of physician assistants dropped from 11 percent to 3 percent in 10 years.

In the selection of students, value continues to be placed on the criterion of previous medical experience, as it was in the profession's beginning; 99.8 percent of entering students have previous health care experience as medical technicians, emergency medical technicians, nurses, nurses aides, or other health care providers. More formalized background in the biological sciences is also increasing.[9] Only 32 percent of the entering students had a bachelor's degree in 1974,[10] but 46 percent had such a degree before entering physician assistant programs in 1985.[11]

When they graduate from the physician assistant educational programs, the new practitioners often go into practice at a site in which they have trained. In fact, the clinical training sites are frequently chosen with that goal in mind. In the early days of the profession, that meant, in most cases, a primary care practice. Physician assistants went into rural community clinics, into general and family practices in out-of-the-way places, and into institutions and prisons. Community health clinics were a major focus of the health care initiatives and made excellent employment sites for physician assistants.

In the mid-1980s, fewer physician assistants are entering primary care medicine, and a variety of specialty practices are seen. This creates both opportunities and problems that are discussed at length in Chapter 9. Their clinical rotations are found in internal medicine, surgery, pediatrics, psychiatry, and emergency medicine practices, in addition to family and general medicine practices.

Until recently, employment of the physician assistant depended largely upon the willingness of individual physicians to hire them. Training programs had to market the physician assistant concept to the initial employers, but gradually the idea became more familiar and employment less problematic. Certainly, familiarity with the concept was critical, but also other factors influenced the acceptability of physician assistants to the medical community. Those who had extra examining rooms, who had patients waiting for long periods of time before being seen, and who were seeing enough patients to warrant extra help were found to be more open to the idea of hiring a physician assistant.[12] Today, employment is not dependent upon the decision of a solo practitioner to hire a physician assistant. Manpower needed in corporate health care settings is determined by factors other than personal choice, and, therefore, the concerns about marketing the physician assistant concept to the family doctor have changed.

QUALITY OF CARE PROVIDED BY THE PHYSICIAN ASSISTANT

Another issue of concern in the profession's first years was the quality of care provided by the physician assistant. Although this concept is difficult to quantify, studies were undertaken to examine if any differences existed between the care provided by the physician and that of the assistant.

Quality of care is particularly difficult to assess using the criterion of how care is given or the results of care. External variables may be as important, or more important, than the events taking place between the patient and the provider. For example, the nutritional status of the patient, his or her health behaviors, or living situations may determine, either totally or in part, the outcome of the medical encounter. Also, many illnesses are self-limiting, and their cures may not be the result of medical intervention. A serious limitation to quality of care studies is that of the inter-observer variability, which is often large. Judgments of appropriate medical behavior in a given case are somewhat subjective in nature, and even qualified examiners of medical records can disagree on what would have been the best course of action in any interaction between patient and provider.

In addition, many reviews of the literature on quality of care have examined all midlevel practitioners and have not separated out the physician assistant. In one study that did address physician assistants solely, however, no significant differences in quality of care from the supervising physician were found.[13]

Efforts were made in the beginning of the movement to develop protocols that would assist physician assistants in examination and treatment of patients. When these protocols were followed, care was found to be particularly satisfactory, but under all circumstances the quality was found to be similar to that from which the standard was derived—the physician's medical care. Little difference was found in accuracy of diagnosis, lab tests ordered, prescriptions ordered or recommended, treatment undertaken, referral patterns to specialists, or other aspects of care.[14]

Patients of physicians using physician assistants in their practices were surveyed in a study conducted in the early 1970s to determine acceptance of the new practitioners. Patients rated the physician assistants very high in terms of technical competence and professional manner. They also said that access to care had been improved with the new health manpower, as well as the quality of care.[15]

CURRENT CHARACTERISTICS OF THE PROFESSION

In 1984 an effort was made to examine the current status of physician assistants and the role they are playing in medical care.[16] All known physician assistants whose names were entered into a master list at the American Academy of Physician Assistants were contacted. Every effort was made to reach potential respondents. From this survey it was determined that 69.4 percent of responding physician assistants remain in primary care practice. Those reporting their specialty as family or general medicine decreased from 49 percent in 1981 to 42.5 percent in 1984.

The community size in which physician assistants practice varies from the largest metropolitan areas to the most rural. Forty percent of physician assistants compared to 16.5 percent of physicians report that they are practicing in communities with fewer than 50,000 inhabitants.[17]

Almost 60 percent of the physician assistants are earning between $20,000 and $30,000 a year. Average salaries in 1984 were $29,663 for males and $24,410 for females. This differential may be due to the preponderance of females in lower paying specialties and the greater number working less than full time.

Respondents stated that they spend most of their time in office or clinic settings. Some are working in hospitals and divide their time among the wards and the emergency, operating, and delivery rooms. Physician assistants are underrepresented in nursing home care and home health care primarily perhaps because of traditional difficulties receiving reimbursement for care provided in these settings and restrictive state practice acts.

Practice settings are changing as new structures of health care provision are being developed. There appears to be a decline in office-based practices since 1981 from 35.9 to 34.4 percent. Hospital-based practices have increased during the same period.

Table 1-3 and Figures 1-1 through 1-6 describe more fully current physician assistant characteristics.

The physician assistant profession was asked by its early proponents to prove that it could provide quality care to the underserved, reduce the perceived manpower shortage in health care, and make the lives of physicians less harried. In the first 10 or 15 years, all of these goals were achieved within the confines of the limited number of personnel being trained in relatively small programs. However, the criteria by which to judge effectiveness changed, and the health care context shifted radically, raising new questions about the role of the physician assistant.

COST-CONTAINMENT EMPHASIS IN HEALTH CARE

By the mid-1970s, it was clear that Medicare, Medicaid, and community-based health initiatives had made an impact on the lives of many Americans. The Health

Table 1-3 Percent Distribution of Physicians and Physician Assistants in 1981

	Physicians	Physician Assistants
General/family practice	22.1	58.3
Pediatrics	8.7	3.4
Ob/Gyn	9.2	2.4
Surgery	12.5	12.3
Other specialties	47.5	23.6
	100.0	100.0

Sources: Association of Physician Assistant Programs. *Secondary Analysis: 1981 National Survey of Physician Assistants,* Arlington, Virginia, June 1984. Robert Wood Johnson Foundation. *Medical Practice in the United States.* Princeton, New Jersey, 1981.

Manpower Act had also filled schools with medical students, and thousands of physician assistants were moving into the community. Using a variety of measures, access to care had never been better. Between 1970 and 1979, the number of active physicians per 100,000 population increased by 25 percent to 190.3. Rural

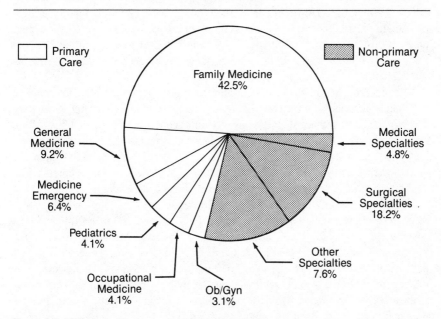

Figure 1-1 1984 Masterfile Survey: Distribution of Physician Assistants Respondents by Medical Specialty. *Source:* Reprinted from *1984 Masterfile Survey* with permission of American Academy of Physician Assistants, © 1984.

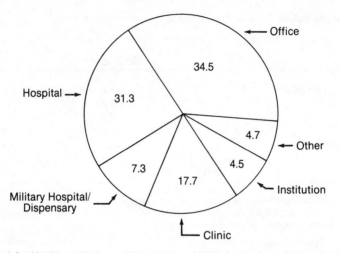

Figure 1-2 1984 Masterfile Survey: Distribution of Physician Assistant Respondents by Practice Setting. *Source:* Reprinted from *1984 Masterfile Survey* with permission of American Academy of Physician Assistants, © 1984.

health care continued to experience manpower shortages with 70.4 physicians per 100,000 population. However, "a marked trend toward equality in the volume of physician visits between the poor and the nonpoor was evident."[18] Life expectancy at birth increased more between 1970 and 1983 than it had in the 20 years prior to 1970 and the gap in life expectancy between blacks and whites in America diminished.[19]

In concentrating on the access issues, the policy makers had not planned adequately for the costs that both increased utilization and government involvement in becoming a third party payer would generate. There had been little advance planning for the impact of the budgetary demands of the federal and state health programs. Nor had there ever been a firm description of what the expanded health care system should look like. In the pluralistic and often fragmented health care domain, each service and benefit was planned independently.

Yet, by 1970, only 5 years after the introduction of Medicare and Medicaid, policy makers were becoming aware of the burgeoning costs of health care. The states were paying for Medicaid services in ever-increasing amounts while the federal government coped with Medicare payments. As the government itself became an insurer, it saw the need to slow health care costs. Health care was driving inflation to the point that President Nixon imposed wage and price controls in the early 1970s and continued them for health care agencies and physicians after they had been lifted for other segments of the economy.[20]

A variety of provider controls were used in the early 1970s. Recognizing that medical doctors were directly involved with much of the health care expenditures,

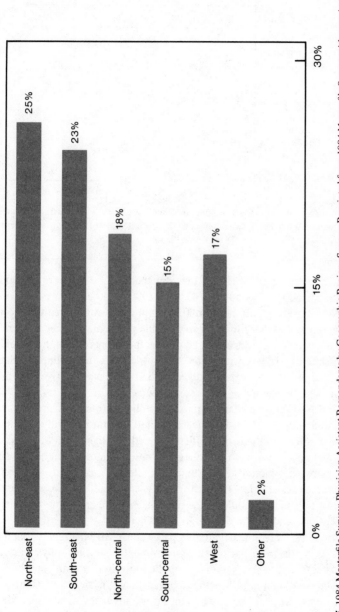

Figure 1-5 1984 Masterfile Survey: Physician Assistant Respondents by Geographic Region. *Source:* Reprinted from *1984 Masterfile Survey* with permission of American Academy of Physician Assistants, © 1984.

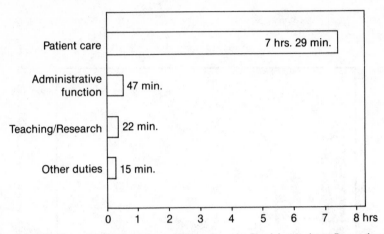

Figure 1-6 1984 Masterfile Survey: Amount of Time Spent by Physician Assistant Respondents in Selected Practice Activities. *Source:* Reprinted from *1984 Masterfile Survey* with permission of American Academy of Physician Assistants, © 1984.

It was estimated by GMENAC that, by the year 2000, there would be 247 physicians per 100,000 population. Using 1990 as a base year, the Committee concluded that there would be 70,000 more physicians than required to provide physician services at that time. To correct this problem, they recommended that medical schools should reduce their class size, the influx of foreign medical school graduates should be severely restricted, and the "need to train nonphysician health care providers at current levels should be studied in the perspective of the projected oversupply of physicians."[22]

The GMENAC Report stated that the number of midlevel practitioners was expected to double by 1990, but they indicated that further study was needed to determine exactly how that would affect the need for physicians. Such variables as specialty and geographic distribution, substitution potential of other practitioners for physicians, productivity, consumer preference, administrative and supervisory parameters, attrition from the health care field, and overlap with other nonphysician providers should all be considered in determining how many midlevel practitioners would be needed.

The profession feared the negative impact of the GMENAC study, but there was no cutoff of funds from the federal government.[23] In fact, physician assistant programs continued to receive student applications in increasing numbers, physician assistants continued to find employment, and physician assistant organizations continued to seek favorable legislative advances. The most significant outcome of the study was a gradual awareness that the profession would have to re-evaluate its mission and redirect its efforts to validate its existence. Now was the time to prove its cost effectiveness.[24]

Even while health care was being expanded in a bold move to provide equity of access, there was an undercurrent of concern about the impact of this expansion of market forces. By the mid-1980s there was enough evidence to alert the public to the need for curbs on health care costs. Whether one looked at percent of gross national product (GNP), federal dollars expended for medical care, or annual percentage of change in the expenditures, a consensus was developing that costs had to be brought under control. The numbers were indisputable. In 1983, health care expenditures in the United States totaled $355.4 billion, an average of $145 per person, and comprised 10.8 percent of the GNP.

The beginning of the current era of cost containment in health care was perhaps signaled by the report of Alain Enthoven on a Consumer Choice Health Plan to then Secretary of HEW Joseph Califano. In this plan, a combination of prepayment options and consumer co-payment would lead to stronger market forces that would bring health care costs down.[25] Although the plan was not supported by the Carter administration, it did not die. It became the focus of heated debate in policy circles and in universities for the next several years.

Under the Reagan Administration, the Enthoven plan received a new interpretation from David Stockman, director of the Office of Management and Budget.[26] Referring to a "neo-conservative" approach, Stockman advocated a move from cost containment on the supply side where strategies had focused on "commanding, controlling, and containing" through use of certificate of need programs and utilization reviews. Instead, more emphasis should be placed on consumer controls. Making the consumer feel the impact of health care expenditures could be accomplished through increasing direct patient payments, providing options for third party reimbursement so that the element of economic choice was reintroduced to the consumer, and limiting the dollar amount of health care coverage provided by employers as a tax-free investment.

Controlling the provider costs under the neo-conservative plan would be attempted through free market risk. The cost of high technology in health care would not be controlled through the certificate of need process, but through the marketing ability of the provider to obtain enough customers to pay for the investment. Health care markets would be viewed as any other market and would not be subject to special treatment.

Of course, the free market as advocated by the neo-conservative approach did not immediately take over the health care enterprise. The idea, however, did have an enormous impact on the way that health care was viewed by the public and policy makers. In the public debate the "right" to health care was replaced by discussions of "good care at affordable cost." Doctors began to see their role as arbiters of a market that was being subsumed by corporate executives as large conglomerates bought out hospitals, clinics, and private practices. Almost overnight the consumer became the "market," and advertising in the form of television commercials, roadside signs, and literature at the supermarket transformed the health care arena from something semisacred to another consumable.

Before the forces of the marketplace completely gained ascendancy, however, voices of concern about access to care and equity for the poor and the medically needy continued to be expressed. The emphasis had shifted, but not without some reminders that in this country neither end of the spectrum can operate without concern for the opposite end.

One of the major concerns raised about equity is the possibility of the rationing of some benefits of health care in the future. Technology is moving at such an enormously rapid rate that new procedures are available almost every month; many of these are very expensive to perform and require equipment that is very expensive to buy. The technological answers seem almost endless, but the resources are finite. Medical students are being trained now to explore the economic consequences of their actions, and experiments are being undertaken around the country to make awareness of cost containment part of the curricula of medical schools.[27]

With the corporatization of medical care, the question arises of who will care for the indigent and the uninsured. Traditionally, there was a cross-subsidy of uncompensated service in which the people able to pay, paid more, and those unable to pay received the benefit of the largesse. Public hospitals and those attached to universities are in danger of going out of business under the stringent systems of payment according to diagnostic-related groups (DRGs). Rationing may very well come into effect on the basis of ability to pay, or we may return to a two-tiered system of health care with hospital wards for the indigent reappearing.[28] There certainly does not seem to be a groundswell among corporate medical groups to assume large-scale responsibility for those who may have difficulty finding a source of payment for health care costs.

Another negative effect of the new mode of health care cost containment may be "patient skimming," in which institutions and corporate medical groups look for the low-cost patient—the one who is middle class, young, and healthy—and ignore those who do not match this picture. Low level of care and insufficient screening and referrals for more costly care are also dangers.

Where does the physician assistant fit into this picture? Will the new trends in health care continue and how will they affect the employment and training patterns of this growing profession? The subsequent chapters provide possible answers to these questions as the adaptation of this new health profession to another side of the health care equation, one that was bound to emerge, is addressed.

NOTES

1. Phillip Lee, "Health Policy and the Health of the Public," *Mobius* 4(1984):104.

2. Arthur M. Okun, *Equality and Efficiency* (Washington, DC: The Brookings Institution, 1975).

3. William Ryan, *Equality* (New York: Random House, 1982).

4. *Physicians for a Growing America: Report of the Surgeon General's Consultant Group on Medical Education*. 1959. U.S. Dept of Health, Education, and Welfare, p. 5.

5. "Not Enough Doctors: What's Being Done," *U.S. News and World Report,* February 19, 1973, p. 53.

6. S.E. Berki, "Health Care Policy: Lessons from the Past and Issues of the Future," *Annals AAPSS* 468(1983):231.

7. Reginald D. Carter and Henry B. Perry, *Alternatives In Health Care Delivery: Emerging Roles for Physician Assistants*. (St. Louis, MI: Warren H. Green, 1984).

8. Association of Physician Assistant Programs, *First Annual Report on Physician Assistant Educational Programs in the United States 1984–85* (Arlington, VA: Association of Physician Assistant Programs, 1985), p. 15.

9. *Report to the President and Congress on the States of Health Personnel in the United States, 1986*. US Bureau of Health Professions, p. 4.

10. Carter and Perry, op. cit., p. 22.

11. Association of Physician Assistant Programs, *Second Annual Report on Physician Assistant Educational Programs in the United States 1985–1986* (Arlington, VA: Association of Physician Assistant Programs, 1986), p. 27.

12. Richard Scheffer, and Dennis B. Gillings, "Survey Approach to Estimating Demand for Physician Assistants," *Social Science and Medicine* 916(1982):1039.

13. Harold C. Sox, "Quality of Patient Care by Nurse Practitioners and Physician Assistants: A Ten Year Perspective," *Annals of Internal Medicine* 91(1979):459.

14. Donald Light, "Physician Surplus and the Future of Physician Extenders," (Unpublished manuscript, 1984).

15. E. Nelson, A. Jacobs, and K. Johnson, "Patients' Acceptance of Physician Assistants," *Journal of the American Medical Association* 228(1974):63.

16. American Academy of Physician Assistants, *1984 Masterfile Survey* (Arlington, VA: AAPA, 1984).

17. Robert Wood Johnson Foundation, *Medical Practice in the United States,* (Princeton, NJ: Robert Wood Johnson, 1981), p. 18.

18. *Health US 1980*. 1980. US Dept of Health and Human Services, Publication No. (PHS) 81–1232, p. 20.

19. Ibid., p. 21.

20. Phillip R. Lee and Carroll L. Estes, "New Federalism and Health Policy," *Annals AAPSS*. 468 (1983):88.

21. *Summary Report of the Graduate Medical Education National Advisory Committee*. 1980. US Dept of Health and Human Services.

22. Ibid.

23. Jerry Weston, "Ambiguities Limit the Role of Nurse Practitioners and Physician Assistants," *American Journal of Public Health* 74(1984):6.

24. Donald Light, op. cit., p. 26.

25. Eli Ginzberg, "The Restructuring of U.S. Health Care," *Inquiry* 22(1985):272.

26. David Stockman, "Premises for a Medical Marketplace: A Neoconservative's Vision of How to Transform the Health System," *Health Affairs* 1(1981):5.

27. John Gordon Freymann, "Teaching Economic Reality to Medical Students," *Business and Health,* April, 1985, pp. 14–18.

28. Glenn Geelhoed, "Ethical Issues in Surgery," *ACS Bulletin,* June 1985, pp. 11–15.

Chapter 2

Negotiated Roles and Alliances

Marshall Sinback is a physician assistant who works in an orthopedic specialty at a Veterans Administration Hospital in Atlanta, Georgia. He is a leader in national and state physician assistant organizations and a recipient of awards and a health policy fellowship for his work on behalf of the profession.

Gretchen Schafft: Is it common for the physician assistant to have to reach an agreement about tasks and responsibilities with a new employer rather than assume that the employer understands the role of a physician assistant?

Marshall Sinback: It depends on whether the physician or the physician assistant is filling a position that has formerly had a physician assistant in a job that has been well defined, or whether the physician assistant is entering a work situation that has never used physician assistants. Second, the degree of role definition also depends on the type of practice. The role of the physician assistant in an institutional setting is probably better defined before the physician assistant actually is brought on board to carry out his or her patient care responsibilities. In a private practice setting, the physician assistant has to do more role development to determine exactly how he or she might function.

Gretchen Schafft: Do you think the physician assistant is prepared to do that? How does a physician assistant learn how to have the self-presence to go in and help the supervising physician, or the administrators of an institution, to do something that is really in the best interest of the physician assistant, the patient, and the practice?

Marshall Sinback: I think there is a certain amount of basic information that prepares the physician assistant to do that role development. That information primarily concerns how the physician assistants are regulated in the particular locale in which they are practicing, and what the standard practice is for the use of physician assistants in that community as well as nationally. Also, physician assistants can understand the appropriate role for the physician assistant within the particular specialty, and how physician assistants are educated, trained, and credentialed. The educational process of becoming a physician assistant should instill an appreciation for the statutes, rules, and regulations within the various states regarding how physician assistants are certified and the basic principle of physician delegation and dependent practice.

Gretchen Schafft: Where do you think the identity that physician assistants feel when they are with other physician assistants comes from?

Marshall Sinback: I think its development begins in the physician assistant training program. Being given the skills by physicians to carry out physician health care responsibilities, having standards of care that are the same as those of the physician, and being given the responsibilities develop the professional *esprit de corps.* I think also in that environment one learns that it is special and unique to be able to do these things. In actual clinical practice and in developing professional relationships with colleagues, a physician assistant can share clinical experiences and share educational experiences through continuing medical education and professional associations as well.

Gretchen Schafft: Are there advantages to having variable definitions of what a physician assistant is at different work sites? Is there some advantage to physician assistants in being flexible enough to change their professional dimensions from site to site?

Marshall Sinback: If there had to be one unique thing to say about the physician assistant role, it is that very thing. Without the flexibility from practice to practice, the physician assistant profession would not be the success that it is today. The concept is based on the fact that one has a fundamental core of knowledge and can adapt it to any given setting. That is one of the very special things about being a physician assistant. One can have a predefined core training and yet be able to develop new skills through further training, academic in some cases, but most of the time, clinical. A physician assistant can develop into areas ranging from family practice to orthopedic surgery, or obstetrics and gynecology. It is absolutely critical in order for the profession to be what it is to have this flexibility. Without that, the physician assistant profession would really probably not exist as it does today. It's fundamental.

Gretchen Schafft: To what extent do you think national laws affect the practice of physician assistants?

Marshall Sinback: National laws to some extent affect physician assistant practice. The things that come to mind, of course, are all familiar. They involve any type of federal insurance program, such as Medicare, and also rules and regulations that are imposed by certifying agencies on various institutions that receive federal funding. Private third-party carriers will often adopt similar policies to reflect national policy. But I would say for the most part that it is state policies, rules, and regulations that primarily affect the physician assistant profession. State statutes, rules, and regulations are really what control and regulate and decide how a physician assistant will function within a particular locality, with very little influence from the federal level. The scope of practice is determined by the states and it determines whether there will be a physician assistant profession.

Gretchen Schafft: Physician assistants are certified nationally but are responsive to various state laws. What is the relationship between these two elements in physician assistant practice?

Marshall Sinback: I would say that certification has to test all possibilities. State laws, rules, and regulations vary from state to state and may be more restrictive or more expansive regarding the profession. So I would say that certification reflects the physician assistant's capabilities more than some state laws. State laws are probably a bit more narrow in scope from locale to locale.

Gretchen Schafft: What other factors develop the physician assistant role?

Marshall Sinback: I think personality and style have a lot to do with it. Being a physician assistant requires a willingness to promote the profession at the same time as practicing it. That requires a certain spirit, public relations, and good will.

NEGOTIATED ROLES AND ALLIANCES

Physician assistants not only are a new type of provider of health care in the United States but also their role is complicated by the profession's placement within a plethora of state and federal laws and regulations and diverse forms of medical supervision.

It is a profession that is defined not only by external rules and regulations to a larger extent than most but also by an individualized definition that each practitioner can mold to suit his or her needs and style. In this chapter, the factors that bear upon the physician assistant role are discussed, and a model of role negotiation is suggested.

A profession is sometimes defined as an exclusive body of tasks and responsibilities not shared by any other profession. In the physician assistant profession, that is certainly not the case. There is overlap with other professions, both up and down the hierarchy of careers. The usual example one thinks of is the overlap with the physician's own role description. The physician assistant is expected to "relieve" the physician of routine, repetitive tasks so that the physician can concentrate time and energy on more complex duties, diagnoses, and treatment modalities. Also, physician assistants are expected to be able to serve in areas where there is a physician shortage. This can mean substituting for the on-site presence of the physician in rural health clinics or inner city health care facilities.

In contrast, the physician assistant is sometimes called upon to substitute for the duties performed by a nurse or a social worker if the staff mix does not allow for a full health care team. In settings where physician assistants work with medical residents, the social service activities not covered by nonclinical staff members are sometimes shunted to the physician assistant, but these are not usually a part of the job description.

The way in which the physician assistant's role is defined determines the cost effectiveness of his or her service, as well as the individual's work satisfaction. Only when the physician assistant labor is substituted for higher priced personnel does that substitution save health care dollars. When that labor is substituted for lower paid workers, the cost of using a physician assistant may be unacceptably high. These concerns regarding care that is both medically sound and uses the health care dollar wisely make the examination of the physician assistant role more than just an academic exercise. How that role is structured is basic to the self-interest of the individual physician assistant and the broader self-interest of the community of patients who may use physician assistant services. Some aspects of the role are nonnegotiable, but beyond those boundaries are areas in which the physician assistant can influence the way this role is developed and can build a very satisfying and individualized career.

NONNEGOTIABLE ASPECTS OF THE ROLE

To understand the nonnegotiable aspects of the physician assistant role, one must answer these questions: Where do the legal stipulations circumscribing the physician assistants' responsibilities originate, how pervasive are they, where are the exceptions to the rules, and how variable are the stipulations from locality to locality?

The legal authorization of the physician assistant profession resides in the state statutes because health care providers have traditionally been licensed and regulated on the state level. In some states the profession is regulated through a well-defined licensing procedure, but in others the process is more flexible and takes the form of a registry or list of practitioners (Table 2-1).

From their inception, the physician assistant training programs intended that the new health practitioners would be providing medical care under the supervision of the physician.[1] This concept came to be known as "dependent practice," but its specifics remained to be interpreted over and over again. Dependent practice, which means that the physician assistant cannot practice without physician supervision, is more closely defined within each state. With the physician assuming responsibility for the performance of medical duties of the physician assistant, the legal responsibilities for that employee also came under the purview of the medical community. The physician assistant profession was regulated through amendments to the state medical practice acts. This legislation began to be considered at the same time that the physician assistant educational programs were first developed.

These amendments to the state practice acts were not instituted uniformly or at one time. They continue to be enacted, changed, and refined. This gradual process is a result of lobbying from the physician assistant interest groups and concerned physicians. Physician assistant educational programs and the state chapters of practicing physician assistants monitor and contribute to this legislative formulation. This lobbying often encounters resistance from legislators who are concerned about maintaining a quality of care standard and do not understand the physician assistant concept or simply choose not to regulate additional health occupations. Some fear that the new health profession could endanger or diminish the quality of patient care. Self-interest on the part of physicians can also come into play. Some feel that the competition from new and cheaper sources of health manpower will not benefit their medical practice.

The advocacy effort for state regulations that allow the physician asssistant to practice in ways that protect the public and enable the use of a full range of training and skills continues to this time. The success of this advocacy effort depends on many factors that the physician assistants themselves can control, including:

Table 2-1 Summary Chart of Selected Provisions from Physician Assistant State Laws and Regulations in 1987

State	Graduation from Approved Program Required	NCCPA Certification Recognized	NCCPA Recertification Required	Scope of PA Practice Determined by		Application Filed by		Temporary Approvals	Prescriptive Privileges
				Physn	Agency	PA	Physn		
ALABAMA	X			X	X		X		
ALASKA	X	X	X	X		X	X	X	X
ARIZONA	X	X	CME required	X	X	X	X	X	X
ARKANSAS	X	X		X	X	X	X		
CALIFORNIA	X	X		X	X	X	X	X	X
COLORADO	X and/or	X		X		X	X		X
CONNECTICUT	X	X		X					
DELAWARE	Regulations under development			X	X				
DISTRICT OF COLUMBIA	X	X		Regulations under development					
FLORIDA	X	X	CME required	X		X		X	
GEORGIA	X	X		X	X	X	X	X	
HAWAII	X	X	X	X		X		X	
IDAHO	X	X	CME required		X	X	X	X	
ILLINOIS	X (or)	X		X	X	X	X	X	
INDIANA	X	X		X		X	X		
IOWA	X	X	CME required	X	X		X	X	
KANSAS	X or equivalent	X	CME required	X		X		X	pending

State				Regulations awaiting approval						
KENTUCKY	X	X		X						
LOUISIANA	X	(or)	X	X	X	X	X	X	X	
MAINE	X	X		X	X	X		X	X	X
MARYLAND	X	X	proposed	X	X	X	X		X	
MASSACHUSETTS	X			X	X	X				in some settings
MICHIGAN	X	X		X	X	X	X	X		
MINNESOTA	X	X	CME required	X	X	X	X		X	X
MISSISSIPPI				X						
MISSOURI	Legislation under consideration			X						
MONTANA	X	X	X	X	X	X	X	X		
NEBRASKA	X	X		X	X	X	X	X		X
NEVADA	X	X	X	X	X	X	X	X		X
NEW HAMPSHIRE	X	X		X	X	X	X	X		
NEW JERSEY	PAs practice only in federal facilities									
NEW MEXICO		X	CME required	X	X	X			X	X
NEW YORK	X (in some cases)			X	X	X				X
NORTH CAROLINA	X (or equivalent)			X	X	X	X			X
NORTH DAKOTA		X		X	X	X		X		
OHIO		X	X	X	X	X		X		
OKLAHOMA	X		CME required	X	X	X	X	X		
OREGON	X			X	X	X	X	X		X
PENNSYLVANIA	X	X	X	X	X	X	X	X		X
RHODE ISLAND	X			X		X		X		pending

Table 2-1 continued

State	Graduation from Approved Program Required	NCCPA Certification Recognized	NCCPA Recertification Required	Scope of PA Practice Determined by		Application Filed by		Temporary Approvals	Prescriptive Privileges
				Physn	Agency	PA	Physn		
SOUTH CAROLINA	X	X	X	X	X		X	see regs	
SOUTH DAKOTA	X	X		X	X	X	X		X
TENNESSEE	X	X		X	X	X		X	
TEXAS	X (or)	X		X	X		X		
UTAH	X	X		X	X	X	X	X	
VERMONT	X or apprenticeship			X	X	X	X	X	X
VIRGINIA	X	X	X	X	X	X	X	X	
WASHINGTON	X			X	X	X	X	X	X
WEST VIRGINIA	X	X	in some cases	X	X	X	X	X	in some settings
WISCONSIN	X	X		X	X	X	X	X	X
WYOMING	X	X		X	X	X	X	X	

Key:

CME   = Continuing Medical Education
NCCPA   = National Commission on the Certification of Physician Assistants
Agency = Regulatory Agency (e.g., board of medical examiners)
Physn   = Supervising Physician

Source: Reprinted from *Physician Assistants: State Laws and Regulations,* 5th ed., with permission of American Academy of Physician Assistants, © 1987.

- the continued interest and motivation of the practitioners and their physician employers and supervisors in each state to monitor the regulating activity within the state
- the education of the medical board and key legislators about the profession and its point of view
- testimony and representation of the profession in state bodies that formulate regulations and laws governing physician assistant practice
- cooperation and communication with the national professional organizations representing physician assistants

Most states have a physician assistant statute that defines what is a physician assistant. Although the state definitions are not uniform, they are similar and usually indicate the educational qualifications and the dependent nature of the practice. In addition, some of the states still subdivide the physician assistant into various categories according to level of training or specialization, but most no longer do so.[2] All states indicate the number of physician assistants who can work at one time under one supervising physician and sometimes the kind of physician who can serve as a supervisor. A physician assistant can have more than one supervising physician.

Registration of physician assistants also varies. States usually register both the physician assistant and the supervising physician, thereby assuring the state that the dependent practice regulations are met. In a few states, the job description of the physician assistant must be registered, as well as the names of practitioners. In these states, physician assistants may try to make their job descriptions as general as possible to allow increased flexibility or may try to update the description to reflect new skills and developments on the job. This is not always possible, because in some states the regulations do not allow this kind of flexibility.

At the federal level, input into the physician assistant profession centers on educational credentialing. The federal government has a vested interest in the physician assistant profession and its potential impact on the nation's health care system. The Comprehensive Health Manpower Training Act of 1970 made possible the establishment of 42 physician assistant training programs, and the Health Professions Educational Assistance Act of 1976 authorized continuation of federal support for physician assistant programs. Federal overseeing, however, was directed at monitoring data from the educational programs and assuring the institution of a responsible and cohesive structure in the development of a new profession.

CREDENTIALING OF PHYSICIAN ASSISTANTS

Accreditation

Credentialing of the physician assistant profession is the responsibility of the Committee on Allied Health Education and Accreditation (CAHEA) of the American Medical Association (AMA), which for more than 50 years has been involved in the accrediting of allied health programs. In 1971, the physician assistant profession had entered into the process by which allied health professions are credentialed by the medical community. This accreditation is grounded in federal law that states that all persons who have responsibility for the delivery of health care services must be accredited by CAHEA.[3] CAHEA establishes the standards for physician assistant program accreditation as described in the document *Essentials of an Accredited Educational Program for the Physician Assistant*. The *Essentials* were first adopted in 1971 and have been revised and updated regularly. The Joint Review Committee on Educational Programs for Physician Assistants monitors the accreditation status of physician assistant programs, conducts on-site visits to sponsoring institutions, and determines the programs' compliance with standards stated in the *Essentials*.

The *Essentials* stipulate the minimum requirements for programs that educate physician assistants. The stated goal of programs for physician assistants, according to the *Essentials*, should be to enable the physician assistant to perform the following services:

1. *Evaluation:* Initially approaching a patient from any age group in any setting to elicit a detailed and accurate history, perform an appropriate physical examination, delineate problems, and record and present the data.
2. *Monitoring:* Assisting the physician in conducting rounds in acute and long-term inpatient care settings, developing and implementing patient management plans, recording progress notes, and assisting in the provision of continuity of care in office-based and other ambulatory care settings.
3. *Diagnostics:* Performing and interpreting, at least to the point of recognizing deviations from the norm, common laboratory, radiologic, cardiographic, and other routine diagnostic procedures used to identify pathophysiologic processes.
4. *Therapeutics:* Performing routine procedures such as injections, immunizations, suturing, and wound care; managing simple conditions produced by infection or trauma; assisting in the management of more complex illness and injury; and taking the initiative in performing evaluation and therapeutic procedures in response to life-threatening situations.
5. *Counseling:* Instructing and counseling patients regarding compliance with prescribed therapeutic regimens, normal growth and development, family planning, emotional problems of daily living, and health maintenance.
6. *Referral:* Facilitating the referral of patients to the community's health and social service agencies when appropriate.[4]

The *Essentials* allow physician assistant educational programs to be developed in medical schools, colleges and universities affiliated with a teaching hospital, medical education facilities of the federal government, or other facilities that can provide the clinically oriented basic science teaching and experience. These facilities must be acceptable to the Council on Medical Education of the AMA, and the curricula that are established must be grounded in clinical medicine. Personal attributes of the clinicians are not neglected as the *Essentials* state, "Throughout, the student should be encouraged to develop basic intellectual, ethical, and moral attitudes and principles essential for gaining and maintaining the trust of professional associates, the support of the community, and the confidence of the patient."[4] Descriptions of the resources needed by the programs, the kind of students to be selected, and related policies are all included in the *Essentials*. The programs are initially accredited by a survey team that visits the institution and makes recommendations to CAHEA. They are later resurveyed for continuing renewal of accreditation.

The U.S. Department of Education recognizes CAHEA as the accreditation agency for physician assistant programs, and it reviews CAHEA decisions on the accreditation of allied health educational programs. It ensures that CAHEA fulfills the responsibilities with which it has been charged. CAHEA's membership is made up of people who have an interest and background in allied health professions and includes both physicians and nonphysicians. Members of the physician assistant profession serve on the Joint Review Committees of CAHEA and assist in the surveys that are done on an ongoing basis.

The Bureau of Health Professions, a federal agency within the Public Health Service with responsibility for the physician assistant profession, serves as a liaison between Congress and the physician assistant education programs. It assists in this communication between Congress and the physician assistant profession by publishing an annual report on the profession, by collecting data on educational programs and practitioners, and by assisting Congress in meeting guidelines for the distribution of funding for educational programs. Personnel in this government office also help staff of the educational programs by interpreting Congressional mandates for funding and serving as an advocate of excellence in curricular development.

Certification

Credentialing of individual physician assistant practitioners was a concern of the federal government within a few years of the first physician assistant graduation.[5] In 1975, personnel of HEW convened a meeting of 25 professional and certifying organizations to develop a study on the potential of certification. They defined certification as

the process by which a nongovernmental agency or association grants recognition to an individual who has met certain predetermined qualifications specified by that agency or association. Such qualifications may include: (1) graduation from an accredited or approved program, (2) acceptable performance on a qualifying examination or series of examinations, and/or (3) completion of a given amount of work experience.[6]

The National Commission on the Certification of Physician Assistants (NCCPA), established in 1974 by representatives of the American Medical Association, major medical specialty groups, and the federal government, took responsibility for the certification process for the profession in 1975. Two charges were given to the NCCPA. First, it had to certify and recertify people who would be called physician assistants to assure the public that the quality of the practitioner met a national standard. Second, the NCCPA had to assure the relevance of the examinations to the practice engaged in by the physician assistant. The initial examination in 1975 was based on primary care practice and did not then take into account the movement of physician assistant specialization. The recertification examination that followed again focused on the primary care role of the physician assistant and was offered after 6 years of practice. Eventually, in 1983, two specialty segments of the recertification examination became available, one in surgery and the other in primary care medicine.

The certification examinations were not required for graduation from physician assistant programs, but came to be recognized by most states as a benchmark of competence. Until 1985, one did not have to be a formally trained physician assistant to become certified provided one could pass the examination. Now, with few exceptions, only graduates of physician assistant programs can gain admittance to the examination. Many places of employment also eventually required certification of the physician assistant as the basis for hiring and retaining employment. Fewer employers require recertification than the initial certification, but in some states, and for some employers, it is a requirement after the 6 years of certification has expired.

The certification of physician assistants was eventually accepted by the profession as a method of gaining public acceptance of a new kind of health practitioner. The National Board of Medical Examiners took responsibility for the development of the examination, and their imprimatur on the exam gave further status to the recipients of the certification. In 1975, a system of mandated continuing medical education (CME) went into effect. To maintain certification, a physician assistant had to gain 100 hours of CME every 2 years. Those credits may be tabulated by the American Academy of Physician Assistants, or by the NCCPA itself.

A consensus about the need for the recertification examination has never developed among physician assistants. The practice of many physician assistants becomes quite specialized after 6 years of practice, and some feel that the primary care focus on the recertification examination is an inappropriate measure of ongoing clinical competence in their practice area. Moreover, mandatory recertification by written examination is not a proven mechanism of validating an individual practitioner's clinical abilities or competence.[7] Arguments in favor of the recertification examination center on the continued need to have public confidence in light of the mobility of physician assistants from one practice to another. Although a physician assistant might be practicing in a specialty, he or she might also move from his or her current employment and take a primary care position again. Without recertification there would be no way of knowing if the physician assistant was still able to function within the primary core of medical practice.

The recertification exam not only tests the individual's knowledge of particular questions, but it also distinguishes between wrong answers and those answered in such a way that they indicate the physician assistant might present a danger to patients. The latter are deemed "unacceptable" answers. In the few cases in which physician assistants have failed the examination and have had a number of unacceptable answers, no legal action by the NCCPA has been taken to strip them of certification. They are simply not recertified until they can perform at an acceptable level. The question of recertification remains volatile for some physician assistants, however, and it is a topic of continued debate and search for new methods.

REFINING THE DEFINITION OF PHYSICIAN ASSISTANT

Physician assistants have always been aware of the need to communicate what goes on in clinical practice with the designers of the educational programs and the certification examination. A new profession needs a particularly strong self-evaluation to determine ways in which it has evolved from the original conception.

Role delineation studies are one way in which information about the new profession could be gathered and analyzed. In 1976, HEW funded a project entitled *The Development of Standards to Ensure the Competency of Physician Assistants*.[8] It combined task analysis surveys of physician assistants with the opinions of experts about what responsibilities should be considered part of the role of the physician assistant and what was tangential to the role. The results of the study became the basis for the continuing medical education program of the American Academy of Physician Assistants (AAPA), as well as its self-assessment examination.

The 1976 study found that the physician assistant role contained three comprehensive areas of competence. These were the *professional role* of the identity of the physician assistant, including the necessary skills and competence to do the work; the *interpersonal role*, which included the ability to communicate effectively; and the *clinical role,* which encompassed the skills and medical knowledge applied to patient problems.

The second role delineation study was conducted by the AAPA in 1985. It showed distinct differences in practice characteristics among physician assistants in the various specialties. However, nine general clusters of activities were common to physician assistance practice across specialty lines. These were:

1. gathering data
2. seeing common problems and diseases
3. conducting laboratory and diagnostic studies
4. performing management activities
5. performing surgical procedures
6. managing emergency situations
7. conducting health promotion/disease prevention activities
8. prescribing medications
9. using interpersonal skills

Protocols were developed to standardize the performance of the physician assistant and to assure physicians and patients that medical treatment would be adequate when provided by the new health practitioner. Protocols are written statements that begin with the patient's presenting complaint and follow stepwise through the questions that should be asked, the tests that should be run, and the medications that should be prescribed. There cannot be a protocol for every situation, but hundreds were written by physician assistant educators and physicians and used extensively in training and practice.

In practice, it is usually not possible for the physician assistant to follow each protocol exactly. A protocol serves as a "security blanket" until the confidence of the provider is sufficient to enable him or her to use the skills and judgment gained with experience. As the employing physicians come to feel comfortable with the work of the physician assistant they are less concerned with the external supports that inform the assistant of correct procedures. They become more concerned with the development of the physician assistant's judgment and critical thinking, particularly in knowing when the patient needs to be referred to the physician.

Through role delineation studies and the development of protocols, the physician assistant profession became codified and set into a structured framework of rules and regulations. This was absolutely crucial to the establishment of the profession. It was necessary in order to convince those early innovators that taking an assistant into the physician's practice would be safe and convenient and would not threaten the patients' confidence.

PRESCRIBING RIGHTS OF PHYSICIAN ASSISTANTS

State laws mandate prescriptive rights and restrictions of health care providers. One of the areas where there is the greatest variation among the roles of physician assistants is in prescribing medication. It varies not only from state to state but also from one health care setting to another. For instance, medical facilities operated by the federal government are able to supersede the state's regulation of prescribing rights and follow their own regulations about which drugs will be in the physician assistant's purview to prescribe.

States that allow physician assistants to prescribe are said to have *enabling legislation*. Such legislation is the focus of much physician assistant advocacy activity at the state level and been achieved slowly through the years as a result of diligent work. In order to support the prescribing rights of physician assistants, both the AAPA and the NCCPA have made efforts through their self-assessment examinations and the certifying examinations to ensure proper training and testing of practitioners in pharmacology. They have also only endorsed prescribing by physician assistants in the states in which there is clear prescriptive authority either through the formation of law or through administrative decision.

There is a difference between prescribing drugs and dispensing them. In almost all cases, the pharmacist dispenses the drugs and acts as a check on the person prescribing them. In states where there is appropriate legislation, physician assistants may prescribe only those drugs that are named in the law. In other states with nonformulary physician control legislation, the physician has the ultimate responsibility for the physician assistant's prescription and must decide which drugs are appropriately in his or her domain to prescribe. The problem with this approach is that the pharmacist is not familiar with each physician's decision and cannot judge the validity of the prescription that comes to the pharmacy in the assistant's name.[9]

States may delegate or regulate the activities of a physician assistant. Under the delegatory system, the physician can delegate authority to the assistant, including the right to prescribe. This right is usually tied to written protocols that must be followed or can only be exercised under the direct supervision of the physician. The physician retains liability for the physician assistant's action. In a regulatory system, the ambiguity of the delegatory guidelines are replaced with specific statutes and statements regarding the physician assistant's education and training, the kind of physician supervision allowed, and the prohibited tasks. These statutes may restrict the prescribing rights of physician assistants in specific ways. Often controlled substances, such as narcotics, are the prohibited pharmaceuticals. In other cases, only certain classes of antibiotics are on the allowable prescription list for physician assistants.

MEANING OF DEPENDENT PRACTICE AND SUPERVISION

The nonnegotiable set of rules and regulations that have just been described is the basic framework of the physician assistant's role. In addition, there are the rules of the workplace. These are developed by the employer, whether it is a single physician practicing in a fee-for-service office setting or a health maintenance organization (HMO) under corporate management. If a physician assistant is employed in one of the Armed Services or by the Veterans Administration, the rules are stated in a very formal job description and available for amendment if a practitioner learns new skills or takes on new responsibilities.

The physician assistant profession is dependent upon the laws and regulations that govern it and define the physician assistant's relationship to the physician. This is the meaning of dependent practice. Unlike the nurse practitioner who in some respects performs in very similar ways to the physician assistant, the physician assistant may not "hang a shingle" announcing an independent practice. A physician is always responsible for the supervision of the assistant. One physician assistant described dependence in this way:

> Dependence, to legislative and regulatory bodies, describes the extent
> of our willingness to be held accountable for our actions. To other health
> care providers, physician assistants' "dependence" states, from our
> first-hand experience, our belief that only someone with a physician's
> training can be safely licensed to practice medicine independently. And
> finally, the public sees our "dependence" as one way we adhere to a
> physician standard of medical care.[10]

The term "dependence" causes problems among physician assistants and is discussed from time to time by their national association committees and state chapters. Periodically, statements and clarifications are issued as internal documents of the AAPA. The reason for the discomfort with the term is the implication that physician assistants are not capable of doing their own work. This is, of course, not the case. Dependence and independence are not very useful terms to use in these descriptions. Their role could be better described as "independent tasks within dependent practice." The dependent practice is a legal necessity as the physician assistant is standing in place of the physician in assuming many of the tasks ordinarily performed by the physician. The legal basis of the profession lies in the supervision of appropriate tasks by the physician.

Issues of independence and dependence are basic to the question of physician supervision of their assistants. For someone outside the profession, the statement that the physician assistant is supervised may bring to mind images of the physician standing at the side of the assistant offering a commentary during an examination of a patient. This does not occur on a regular basis. Supervision by the physician can take many forms, some of which allow the physician assistant more autonomy than others.

In outpatient care, the supervision is provided by the physician who is usually on-site but is busy seeing other patients. The physician assistant is assigned particular patients as a regular caseload or is assigned a class of patients as a primary responsibility. For instance, the physician assistant may have a "panel" of patients or a group of patients who have been examined initially by the physician who has then determined that they are appropriate for the physician assistant to follow. One form of supervision occurs when the physician conducts the initial examination and sees the patient periodically or as needed thereafter. If a problem arises that seems too difficult for the physician assistant to handle between these physician examinations, the patient is immediately referred to the supervising physician. This particular form of supervision is often found in HMOs. Every time the physician assistant sees the patient, the notes from the visit are read by the physician who signs them at the end of the day.

Closer supervision may occur while the physician is learning about the capabilities of the physician assistant. Under these circumstances, he or she may drop in on the patient before the patient leaves the office to double-check the diagnosis and treatment plan of the physician assistant. Another form of more immediate supervision occurs when the physician checks the patient chart before the patient leaves the office to see if there are any problems that should be handled before the patient leaves. Almost invariably, as the physician and his or her assistant come to know one another well, the supervision becomes less rigid and the physician assistant knows what signs and symptoms require a quick consultation with the physician while the patient is being examined.

In rural health care, it is often the physician assistant who is the primary provider of health care, with a physician available by telephone or a hospital awaiting emergencies that cannot be handled in the office. Under these circumstances, the physician is on-site only rarely, depending on the state laws governing physician assistant practice. The charts are examined on a weekly basis or even less often, and the physician assistant must make judgments about the appropriate care for the patient. This is a great deal of responsibility for the practitioner and may not suit every physician assistant. This kind of supervision may also be found in clinics run by nonprofit social agencies in the inner city and staffed by volunteers. Here resources are meager and care is provided for maintenance of such chronic conditions as arthritis and hypertension or acute care is provided for common infections. Physicians are in short supply in these health care settings, and the physician assistant has the opportunity to provide needed medical care in a somewhat autonomous way.

The number of physician assistants that can be supervised by one physician is a question that arises in some institutional settings. Prison settings often do not have adequate physician labor and rely heavily upon physician assistants. In order to protect their integrity as health care clinicians, physician assistants have had to request, in some instances, more supervision in order to assure their own ability to provide the care that they have promised to provide.

Supervision in Nursing Homes

Supervision in nursing homes has been an issue over the years. Must the physician be on-site at all times? In some states, the regulations have imposed this unrealistic requirement, and, because it is virtually financially impossible to have a full-time physician on the staff of smaller homes, the physician assistant is excluded from participating in the provision of much-needed care. When physician assistants are not allowed to prescribe common pharmaceuticals, their usefulness also drops below the point of providing necessary returns for the nursing home managers.

Massachusetts was one of the first states to pass legislation allowing the physician assistant to work semi-independently in the nursing home environment with day-to-day supervision by the physician conducted over the telephone. In this system, the physician assistant or nurse practitioner has the authority to prescribe medications and is the primary practitioner in the nursing home setting. He or she contacts the physician when problems arise and assists the physician on rounds during the physician's periodic visits that are required by law. The success of this system depends on the involvement of the physician with the physician assistant and the interest in quality patient care being maintained on a high level. The physician must be available to answer the telephone when the physician assistant raises a question about a patient's status and must be available to come to the home or meet the patient at the hospital if the situation warrants. The cost savings of this system in Massachusetts are significant.[11] News of this success encourages broader employment of midlevel practitioners in that state and in others.

ROLE NEGOTIATION FOR THE PHYSICIAN ASSISTANT

It is in the physician assistant's best interest to understand the boundaries of the role very clearly and to evaluate thoroughly the kind of practice in which he or she will be most comfortable. Useful steps can be taken in order to accomplish these objectives.

One might wonder why the physician assistant profession has not taken a stand in favor of independent practice as have the nurse practitioners. The philosophical roots of the two professions are very different, although in many instances their actual performance of tasks is almost identical. Nursing is grounded in the belief that it is different from medicine and is based on a different set of skills. Therefore, the physician cannot supervise the competence of the completion of those tasks in a field about which he or she has no particular knowledge. Nursing believes this competence must be judged by a nurse. This concept sets the groundwork for the nurse supervisor and a layer of independent nursing administration in most large institutions.

The physician assistant by definition is doing much of the work of the physician. Who is in a better position to judge the competence of the performance of those responsibilities than the physician? This concept is the basis on which the profession is grounded and has a political reality of its own as well. The agencies that certify the professionals who call themselves physician assistants would not feel comfortable with independent practice for physician assistants and would not sanction it. Any move to independent practice would endanger the position of the profession and possibly have a negative effect on patient care.

Supervision of physician assistants has been described as prospective, concurrent, and retrospective. *Prospective* supervision refers to elements of supervisory policy established prior to the physician assistant seeing patients. *Concurrent* supervision refers to supervision while the physician assistant is actively functioning on the job. *Retrospective* supervision deals with performance review.[12] Obviously prospective supervision plays a part in every case in which the physician and his or her assistant decide how the work will be allocated between them. In some cases there may be no concurrent supervision, but there is always retrospective supervision as the physician checks the charts of the patients that the assistant has seen and decides if the care has been appropriate. The certification and recertification processes also add to the prospective and retrospective supervisory structure.

The physician assistant, to a greater extent than other allied health practitioners, can influence the duties and responsibilities that will fall into his or her domain. In order to do this effectively, the physician assistant must be able to assess individual preferences, learn the state regulations, know the job market, and be an astute judge of employers.

First, the physician assistant must learn the state laws and the regulations governing practice. If there is a choice of states in which one could practice, a thorough study of all of the possible state laws should be made. This can be done easily by examining a copy of the *Physician Assistants: State Laws and Regulations* published periodically with the latest information by the AAPA. Most physician assistants would choose to practice in states with "friendly" laws, such as prescriptive practice allowances and flexible supervisory regulations. However, some physician assistants may like a more restricted environment, and they should choose such a state if that is their preference.

Next, the physician assistant about to make a career move should assess what particular skills and interests he or she brings to the position. Was the physician assistant educational program a specialty-oriented program, or was it geared to general practice? What prior job experience has the physician assistant had, and what elements have been most satisfying in previous employment settings? Are there any particular skills that could be brought to the employer's attention that would enhance the working conditions or the wage?

Someone contemplating a career choice should then determine which settings in the area are open to physician assistants. If physician assistants have hospital privileges in the community or opportunities to work in nursing homes, obviously, there will be expanded job opportunities. In such cases, the physician assistant should learn who in the corporate structure makes the hiring decisions in these settings. Initial inquiries can help determine who the key people are in institutional hiring. Also, the state chapters of the physician assistant organizations can be very helpful.

If a physician assistant does not have a choice of employment locales and is not pleased with the restrictions placed on the practice by state laws, there is still the opportunity to find an exemption through alternative practice sites. For instance, the federal Veterans Administration may have a facility within one's geographic area, and their rules and regulations are well defined and accepting of physician assistant practice. Often in a rural community, exceptions are made to the otherwise more stringent supervisory rules.

The physician assistant has to take responsibility in many cases for informing the health care employers of state regulations governing midlevel practitioners. Not all employers will be familiar with the physician assistant concept and may be hesitant to use this kind of health care personnel. It is helpful to have printed materials describing the role of the physician assistant in that particular state to send to a prospective employer or bring to an interview. State licensing boards and state physician assistant associations often have such information, or it can be obtained in a more generic form from the AAPA national office.

Physician assistants may want to impress upon potential employers the following facts:

- Legislation passed by the 1986 Congress allows for Medicare Part B coverage of physician assistant services in nursing homes, hospitals, and as assistants at surgery.
- Most malpractice cases occur when there is poor communication between patients and their doctors. Physician assistants can spend more time with patients in education and explanation. This activity can serve as a check against malpractice claims.
- Physician assistants can provide patient continuity in inpatient settings where residents and interns will have regular turnover.
- Physician assistants act as a backup to the physician, allowing the physician to address the serious problems more intently and relieving him or her of the minor and chronic patient care.

EMERGING ROLES FOR PHYSICIAN ASSISTANTS

There is virtually no unemployment among physician assistants. In fact, there is a physician assistant shortage throughout the country, and the choices are wide for individuals. As the profession becomes more widely known, there is more latitude in choosing a particular position and more options become available. For instance, in many inpatient settings the position of physician assistant coordinator is in place.[13] This person is responsible for hiring, training, and deploying physician assistants throughout the facility and arranging inservice training. He or she is in close communication with the medical director about the direction of patient care and needs of the facility. Management tasks may be interspersed with clinical responsibilities.

Another role that is developing for physician assistants is that of case manager. This person follows the patient through care to ensure proper placement in the hospital, nursing home, or rehabilitation center. Patients followed by the case manager are usually geriatric or chronic long-term care recipients of health care, and their insurance coverage, need for services, and interaction with families present multiple problems to standard medical practice. Such a specialist serves as a patient advocate, as well as the practice's coordinator of quality patient care.

The physician assistant has often been described as being in a closed system without a good career ladder to other employment opportunities. This characterization may no longer be accurate. More administrative and managerial positions are becoming available as the early practitioners mature. Teaching positions are also available, as well as opportunities to enter specialties with further specialty training. Currently, there are postgraduate physician assistant specialty training programs in emergency medicine, neonatology, pediatrics, surgery, and occupational health. Physician assistants can obtain master's degrees in public health, public administration, and business, all of which can be productively wedded to the initial physician assistant training.

CONCLUSION

The physician assistant is in dynamic alignment with the supervising physician, the corporate employer, and the state regulatory agencies. The individual who is clear about his or her priorities, understands his or her own personality and style of work, and can analyze the variety of health care settings in a given location will be in an excellent position to maximize job satisfaction. In the search for the best employment opportunity the physician assistant should ask the following questions:

- How is the supervision arranged in this position?
  Prospective supervision: To what extent is the job governed by state laws and

by facility regulations? Does the job description describe the nature of the supervision? Is the nature of the supervision in concordance with state regulations?

Concurrent supervision: Has the physician worked with a physician assistant before? Is the style of on-site supervision satisfactory to me? Does the physician seem to be flexible?

Retrospective supervision: Will I receive feedback on my notes and patient charts? Are the expectations clear on both sides about my capabilities? Will I have a chance to learn new skills on the job and be given more responsibility (and salary) over time?

- Is there a health team in operation at this site? If so, will the position of physician assistant be clear to everyone? How can that clarity be ensured?
- Will the salary and benefits reflect any on-call hours that are expected of me?
- Will I be given time to take CME and will I receive reimbursement for attending out-of-town meetings to advance my career?

The physician assistant can have a fulfilling career if he or she has a good understanding of the health care system. Success will be dependent on the skills brought to the job, the interactions in the workplace, and the ability to continue professional growth. The need continues to educate both patients and medical staff about the profession with clarity and self-confidence. The outlook is bright for successful role negotiation.

NOTES

1. Henry C. Miller, *Review and Analysis of State Legislation and Reimbursement Practices of Physician's Assistants and Nurse Practitioners,* Final Report Contract No. HRA 230-77-0011 (Department of Health, Education and Welfare, PHS, NCHSR, 1978), p. 75.

2. *New Members of the Physician's Health Care Team: Physician's Assistants* (Washington, DC: National Academy of Sciences, 1970), pp. 3–6.

3. William R. Burrows, "Allied Health Education and Accreditation," *Journal of the American Medical Association* 256 (1986):1606–1610.

4. American Medical Association Council on Allied Health Education and Accreditation, *Essentials of an Accredited Educational Program for the Physician Assistant* (Chicago: American Medical Association, 1985), p. 2.

5. *Report on Licensure and Related Health Personnel Credentialing.* US Department of Health, Education and Welfare, 1971.

6. Ibid., p. 7.

7. R.W. Jarski and J.J. Heinrich, "Recertification: Options for Physician Assistants," *Physician Assistant* 10 (1986):132.

8. American Academy of Physician Assistants, *The Development of Standards to Ensure the Competency of Physician Assistants* (Arlington, VA: AAPA, 1979).

9. Burdeen Camp, "Prescribing Rights of Physician Assistants" (Unpublished manuscript).

10. Charles G. Huntington, "On Dependence," *Physician Assistant* 9 (October 1985):6–14.

11. Gretchen Schafft and Barbara Rolling, *Physician Assistants Providing Geriatric Care*, January 1987, HRP 090702, p. 6.

12. John Trimbath, *American Academy of Physician Assistants Memorandum*, October 18, 1985, p. 2–3.

13. Schafft and Rolling, *op. cit.*, p. 41.

Chapter 3

Provision of Care to the Underserved: The Physician Assistant's Role

Carl Toney and Claudio Lima are physician assistants who have been active in the AAPA's Minority Affairs Committee. They are practicing clinicians who spend a great deal of time working on increasing minority representation in the profession and increasing services to the poor. In this interview, both men discuss the state of health care for America's poor.

Carl Toney: When you look at most state health manpower resource statistics, virtually every state has at least some areas that are severely underserved or, in some cases, not served at all. Despite the fact that there are a greater number of health care providers, both physician and nonphysician providers, we still are facing a major problem, particularly when you look at it in terms of distribution of those manpower resources.

Claudio Lima: I vouch for what Carl is saying. Furthermore, health care is not provided in the same way to the poor and the nonpoor. The poor have much less access, and unless there is a specific program they can feel comfortable with, where they can go and receive medical care, it is very difficult for them to obtain it. My experience is mostly with migrant populations. For a while I thought their health care was improving, but lately the trend is to limit access to migrant farm workers and generally poor populations. Equality of access to primary care is arguable, but with special referrals and specialty care, there is a significant problem because the poor do not have medical insurance. Even if you work in a community health center or a migrant clinic, as I have, you can deliver some type of primary care at a feasible level, but it depends on the will and sometimes the wits of the medical community to provide specialty care.

Carl Toney: I would certainly agree with Claudio's comments. In addition, I think there are two other factors that you have to consider when you look at whether there is a two-tiered system of health care. Even assuming the poor have access to care, they do not have much choice in selecting a health provider. If you are middle class you have options in terms of the type of care that you are going to get: what level, what quality, and often the sequence of that care. When you are poor, you receive most of your care in clinics or municipal hospital settings.

Issues and practices of preventive medicine are virtually unheard of in services to the poor, and there is little commitment, I believe, on the part of the medical community in general to become involved in those areas when working with the poor. And so you are dealing with a group that comes to the system late, has difficulty gaining access to the system, tends to have more complicated problems—both medical and other social-economic problems that are going to affect the medical care delivered—and finally, as I said before, has little power or control over how the medical system responds to their individual and collective needs.

I personally believe, having been not only a teacher but also a practitioner within the profession, that the physician assistant concept, and the actual practice of physician assistants, is a very concrete answer to this problem. Not that it is by any means a definitive answer. They are a group of individuals who are clinically trained in the areas where they are needed and who philosophically are committed to providing care to those who need it. They are willing. The problems we face that hinder care from being provided to the degree that it could or should be tend to be regulatory, legislative, or economic issues that are outside of the control of the physician assistant professional.

Claudio Lima: I think minority physician assistants in particular are interested in serving minority and low-income patients. Sometimes that sentiment doesn't go across the board, especially as we witness the development now of more fields where physician assistants can almost super-specialize. When we are talking of access to medical care for the poor and indigent, I personally hope that we won't move away from the old concept for which we all worked so hard: the original concept of service.

Carl Toney: Physician assistants, in general, have a commitment to provide care to everyone, and, in particular, to those who are in need. That need may be rooted in ethnic issues, geographic issues, or economic issues. I think you find in our profession, as in other professions such as law or nursing, that people who come from ethnic minority backgrounds tend to want to provide their particular service in their own communities or at least to their own ethnic group. I don't think it is the minority physician assistant's role to assume the responsibility in full, but I think in a practical sense there is a great human interest generated in minorities for their own ethnic groups. They also bring the advantage of a greater understanding of social, cultural, and religious issues that affect health care.

Claudio Lima: I think Carl is right and I would add that communicating in the same language is an advantage. A nonminority provider can do an excellent job working in ethnic minority communities, but the physician assistant profession needs to keep training minority practitioners so that they are well represented in our ranks.

THE PHYSICIAN ASSISTANT'S ROLE

Physician assistants were brought into the family of health care professions primarily to increase the scope of clinical services to people who fell outside the mainstream of health care. Although physician assistant numbers have not increased enough in the 20 years of their existence to enable them to penetrate into every community nor answer every need of medically underserved groups, they have disproportionately served the socially, economically, and geograpically isolated people in this country. For instance:

- Thirty-six and a half percent of patients of physician assistants are minorities.
- Nineteen percent of their patients are poor or very poor.
- Thirty-two percent of their patients are over the age of 65.
- Forty percent work in rural areas or small towns.[1]

How does a health profession maintain service to the underserved as a focus when self-interest draws people to higher salaries in institutions and offices serving the mainstream population? First, the basic and traditional tenets of the profession must be taught in the educational programs in both the didactic and the clinical phases. This, in fact, is the case in nearly all physician assistant programs. The innovative spirit, commitment to service, psychosocial orientation, and awareness of the disadvantaged are important components of the heritage of the profession. Second, students who display an empathy with a broad range of patients must be selected into programs. Therefore, the educational programs must continue to recruit a heterogeneous student body, must find methods that retain these students through successful graduation and certification, and must then encourage them to spend part of their careers, at least, in providing health care to the underserved.

This chapter discusses the progress that has been made in bringing care to all segments of our society, the problems that remain, and the efforts that must be made by the physician assistant profession to provide better access to care. Although these issues have not been the center of attention among health professionals in the past few years, they will predictably emerge again if our thesis is correct that equity concerns seldom lag far behind market interests.

EARLY CONCERN FOR THE UNDERSERVED

Ethnic and racial minorities were well represented among physician assistants in the early years of the profession and were, perhaps, responsible for much of the fulfillment of the profession's promise to serve the poor and minority populations.

Many of these minority group members were returning veterans of the Vietnam conflict. They brought expertise gained as medics on the battlefield to the class-room where in a relatively short time they were able to be trained to provide clinical care to civilian populations as they had previously provided it to military personnel. Opportunities existed in the early days of the physician assistant training programs to place graduates in a variety of health care settings in poor and underserved areas. The National Health Service Corps employed some of these physician assistants, and community clinics, migrant clinics, jails, and public institutions hired others.

By the 1980s, a combination of factors contributed to a decrease in the proportion of physician assistants who chose to work in these areas of need. First, the growing recognition of the profession opened many new employment areas, both clinical and administrative, to physician assistants, and some of these new areas were highly paid. Second, the funding for the neighborhood health centers and the National Health Service Corps decreased drastically, and the possibility that physician assistants would find employment through these channels declined. Third, programs that encouraged the development of more health care personnel came to a halt or slowed considerably after the GMENAC report of 1980.[2] A projected surplus of physicians indicated that no further recruitment was neces-sary. Physician assistants no longer were viewed as an answer to the problem of underutilization of health care, but rather part of the problem of a surplus of clinicians. However, perceptions of supply and demand are not always matched by reality. What evidence exists that there is or is not a continuing problem of service provision in American health care?

INDICATIONS OF INCREASED ACCESS TO CARE

Before Medicare and Medicaid, many people in the United States had no health insurance at all or had only very limited benefits. They either negotiated on a personal basis with their physicians for their care, sought care but ignored their medical debts, or neglected to seek help for their medical problems. Soon after the introduction of the Social Security amendments, it appeared that the gap virtually disappeared between the "haves" and the "have nots." However, the places in which care was given remained different for the poor and the middle class, with the poor continuing to depend on emergency room care and the middle class finding private care. There remained the difference in quality of care that these different settings infer, but the number of office visits and hospitalizations became more frequent for the poor than for the nonpoor. The poor in 1975 saw physicians 18 percent more frequently than the nonpoor and had more surgical procedures performed in hospitals than the nonpoor.[3]

Today, Medicare covers almost all of the people over the age of 65, as well as many others who fit one of the nonaged categories of recipients. Medicaid reaches fewer individuals as a proportion of all those in need because it is based on state regulations that count some medically needy into the program and some out. One state, Arizona, chooses not to participate in the Medicaid program at all.

In the years since Medicaid was established, infant mortality has been cut in half, and death rates from influenza, pneumonia, diabetes, and tuberculosis have declined significantly. The age-adjusted overall mortality rate for Americans has been reduced 20 percent.[4]

CONTINUING PROBLEMS IN RECEIVING MEDICAL CARE

Although Medicare and Medicaid enabled the aged and poor to take advantage of new health care resources and utilization figures for physician and hospital services rose, the gradual reductions in coverage in those programs have brought into question the extensiveness of the care received and whether it has truly met the needs of the nation. The proportion of the country's poor receiving Medicaid has declined, and Medicare recipients have been asked to pay so many of the charges for services that they are now paying as much for health care out of their own pockets as they were before the program was enacted. For example, between 1975 and 1983, the proportion of low-income people covered by Medicaid dropped from 63 percent to 46 percent. This was a period of time when the ranks of Americans living at or below 125 percent of the federal poverty level rose 27 percent.[5] Only 40 percent of the children in poverty are covered by Medicaid. Their problems are so significant that they are discussed separately.

All states are required to provide aid to recipients of Supplemental Security Income and Aid to Dependent Children, but that leaves many intact families, childless couples, and single adults outside the safety net. Among those are people who suffer catastrophic illness or long-term disability, those who are unemployed, and those who are uninsured though employed. In 1983, 14 percent of the families in the United States believed that they needed medical care, but could not afford to receive it.[6]

Unemployment almost always results in the loss of insurance and the resulting deficits of medical care. Harvey Brenner of the Johns Hopkins School of Hygiene and Public Health has documented the devastating effects on mortality and morbidity of unemployment.[7] When unemployment is disproportionately distributed among the population, with higher rates among minority groups or among certain age groups, then it is clear that these are the groups who will be among the most at risk for medical indigence. Currently, the majority of the uninsured are white, but the percentages of the uninsured as a proportion of the ethnic group are higher for blacks and Hispanics.

Fifteen percent of Americans are without insurance of any kind in 1986. Of those who are insured, many do not have adequate benefits to cover serious or long-term illness. Many jobs are dependent upon continuing good health, and illness can mean a simultaneous loss of job and insurance.

There is a growing number of employed people without insurance. These include those who are employed sporadically throughout the year or who work part-time. Some are in higher income jobs, but most are receiving close to the minimum wage. They are in no position to pay for private insurance. Indeed, those who do insure themselves without employer pools of insurees pay top dollar for their policies, which then do not provide the coverage of larger plans that are offered through places of work.

Those who are uninsured bring that status to those around them. Their dependents are also without protection. It is startling to realize that three-quarters of the uninsured are employed individuals and their dependents.[8]

All indicators of usage of care decline for the uninsured. There is a lower usage of pharmaceuticals, fewer physician visits, and fewer hospitalizations. Another result of uncompensated care that is receiving increased attention is the phenomenon of "dumping" in which private hospitals refuse to admit indigent patients for care, but send them to public hospitals. In 1984, hospitals furnished $5.4 billion of care for which they were not compensated.[9] This figure does not represent the commitment on the part of hospitals to provide charity because it also includes bad debts, bills that could not be collected. Public hospitals continue to care for the majority of the uninsured. As private hospital chains gain ascendancy in the health care marketplace and public hospitals become less available to the poor, increased problems of access will occur.

The burden of the uninsured on hospitals is greater now under the system of prospective payment because it is more difficult to cross-subsidize patients. In the traditional fee-for-service reimbursement system, when the more financially able patients paid a little more, they covered the costs of care for those less able. With the diagnosis-related group (DRG) system in place, there is a more rigorous assessment of actual costs, and it is more difficult for hospitals to account and provide for the care of the poor.

Many suggestions have been made to develop a system that would cover the costs of the uncompensated care in hospitals. A user fee on patients, sometimes called a "sick tax," would accomplish in a visible way what cross-subsidizing had previously accomplished behind the scenes. Some object to this plan as placing an unfair burden on people who are already facing the high copayments of medical care.

Many in the public health community feel that Medicaid must be expanded to include all of the medically needy. The additional expense could be offset by taxes on cosmetics, tobacco, or alcohol or by employer taxation on health care benefits.

These advocates feel that the health care of the population is a right and should not be allocated in a way that leaves some on the sidelines.

There has been increasing discussion of the creation of state pools for insurance coverage. At the state level, taxation could provide medical funds for uncompensated care. Letting states decide how much coverage to provide is congruent with the New Federalism of the Reagan administration as the movement of shifting fiscal decision making to the states is sometimes called. It brings the problem of unequal coverage again to the fore, however, as some states will provide only the minimum and others will be unfairly burdened with generous programs that may even attract those with severe medical problems to the state.

The uninsured make up a risk pool for the health providers that, at times, threatens the fiscal viability of the health care institutions in areas of intense need.

THOSE MOST AT RISK

Those who are most visible to city dwellers are the homeless who have increasingly populated the streets of the urban centers throughout the country. The National Institutes of Mental Health estimate that in 1985 there were 2 million homeless people without a permanent residence.[10] Many of these people are suffering from mental illness and have been released from institutions without places to go in the community.

Reform movements of the 1970s led to rulings that a patient cannot be held against his or her will if there is insufficient evidence that the patient will be a danger to self or others. Declining budgets of institutions provide further motivation to follow these rulings perhaps beyond their original intent.

It is a mistake, however, to fail to recognize the heterogeneity of the homeless population. Twenty-two percent of the homeless, by some estimates, are children, as increasing numbers of the poor are losing affordable housing and moving to the streets.

People on the street suffer from a wide variety of ailments. Many of their problems are a result of the lives that they lead, and others are problems that they might have had under other circumstances but that are intensified by exposure to the elements. Dermatologic problems, such as impetigo, scabies, and leg ulcers, are the most common ailments found by health care workers who have investigated the health status of street people. Musculoskeletal problems, angina, tuberculosis, and cancer are also commonly seen.[11]

The indigent and low-income populations have traditionally sought medical care in emergency rooms, which have assumed that there is an unlegislated right of the population to have emergency treatment. Antidumping laws have had to be enacted by states and the federal government to translate that assumption into practice in the face of the health care constraints of the 1980s. Community health clinics also provided care to the needy following their inception in the 1960s. Unfortunately, they have also been financially threatened. In 1982, 250 community health centers closed, and many of the programs that they had provided have been curtailed.[12]

Children are particularly affected adversely by poor access to health care. Children are even vulnerable before birth to all the prenatal influences of diet and lifestyle of the mother. The tragedy of "children having children" is increasingly a contentious issue as the community is divided between those who believe that measures must be taken to prevent conception and birth of unwanted children and others believing that behavioral change, not medical intervention, is needed.

The facts are very clear, however; children in poverty are a growing population that is at grave risk for illness and disability.

- One in five children lives in a female-headed household.
- There were more than 100,000 black children in foster care in 1980.
- In 1982, 14.2 percent of births were to women under the age of 20, and almost 40 percent were to unmarried women.
- In 1980, 66 percent of pregnancies for women between the ages of 15 and 19 were unintended.
- More than one child out of five was living in poverty in 1983.
- One-fourth of the children under age 6 were not covered by health insurance in 1977.[13]

Black children are most at risk. By every health measure, their status is less secure than that of white children. It is not ethnicity, however, that is the cause of this increased risk. It is poverty. Poverty is perpetuated when the pathways to the middle class are blocked by inadequate education, inadequate employment opportunities, neighborhoods that are filled with illicit activities and drugs, and hopelessness in finding a way out of the poverty cycle. Large numbers of middle-class blacks are recognizing the need to continue their historical involvement in community enrichment as the environment becomes more hazardous for the young.

The health status of the minority population of the United States was addressed by the Department of Health and Human Services (DHHS) in the early 1980s. It found that, despite remarkable strides in the health status of Americans in this century, there is still a disparity between the health of blacks and whites.

- There remains a gap of 5.6 years in the life expectancy of blacks and whites.
- Blacks have twice the infant mortality rate as whites.
- Cancer incidence is 25 percent higher for black males than for nonminority males.

- Black males are ten times more likely to die from hypertension than white males and twice as likely to die from stroke.[14]

Causes of excess death, which was the measure used by the DHHS study to look at the health status differentials between whites and minorities, found six areas that were significant: heart disease and stroke, homicide and accidents, cancer, infant mortality, cirrhosis, and diabetes. There are two ways of approaching these data. First, one could say that all of these health problems are amenable to health promotion/disease prevention activities and that self-help may be the most efficacious way to lessen the disparity between blacks and whites. Second, one could make the case that outside help is needed to provide the resources that make the self-help possible. Health care professionals who have looked at the data have taken both approaches, and there has been some debate about the meaning of the findings.

Certainly, the extension of health promotion activities to minority communities is vital, but some wonder if handgun control could also be considered such an activity. Cigarette advertising is targeted on minority communities where it finds a welcome reception. More influence must be exerted to balance the allure of smoking presented by the tobacco companies to the black community with the dangers presented by smoking. The same is true for "junk foods," which currently enjoy excellent sales in communities where convenience stores are more likely to be found than full-scale food markets.

Other suggestions made by DHHS to improve minority health are as follows:

- continue to support or fund existing health programs that have been successful
- improve data collection and interpretation of data regarding specific minority groups
- direct resources to prevention activities for high-risk minority populations
- increase funding for health education programs and research on health disparities
- incorporate bicultural/bilingual services into health programs
- network with private medical and social communities
- develop public education programs and other programs encompassed by the *1990 Objectives for the Nation*.[15]

The report suggests that minority health care providers play an important role in bringing adequate health care to the community. In the case of the community whose language is not English or a culture that is distinctive from the mainstream, such as Indian communities, health care providers who have knowledge and understanding of their patients can be much more effective in providing health care that promotes good health.

MINORITY REPRESENTATION IN THE PHYSICIAN ASSISTANT PROFESSION*

Physician assistants from racial and ethnic minority groups are vital to the viability of the physician assistant profession. At the same time that this has become recognized within the profession, demographic data indicate that black participation in the physician assistant profession is decreasing.

The 1984 Masterfile Survey conducted by the AAPA showed that there are significant differences in practice characteristics among physician assistants who identify themselves as belonging to one of several ethnic/racial groups. These differences play an important role in patterns of health care provision to segments of the community that are traditionally underserved. It is therefore important to examine the changing ethnic/racial composition of the profession and find ways to strengthen minority representation among the numbers of graduate physician assistants.

Studies of minority participation in the health professions were more topical in the 1970s than in the 1980s.[16-20] The ideological climate of the 1970s still supported an interest in rectifying what was believed to be an underrepresentation of minorities in health careers and an inadequate distribution of health manpower. Many believed that a clear link existed between the numbers of minorities employed in the health professions and the adequacy of health care resources found in minority communities.[21-24]

Various programs instituted by the government during the late 1960s and early 1970s addressed ways to increase minority representation in the health professions and to bring increasing numbers of economically, geographically, and socially isolated people into health care systems. Such programs as the National Health Services Corps, the Health Professions Educational Assistance Act, Area Health Educational Centers, the Health Professions Scholarship Program, and funding of community health centers and urban clinics worked toward these goals. Medicare and Medicaid were thought to be sufficient to finance the increased costs of this health care.

The creation of the physician assistant profession itself was tied not only to ideas of improving access to care but also to providing a career ladder to people who had

---

*The following section was adapted with permission from "Trends of Practice among Minority Physician Assistants: Their Importance to the Profession" by G.E. Schafft from Proceedings of the 1986 Annual Meeting of the Association of Physician Assistant Programs. Paper presentation, May 23–29, 1986, pp. 12–22.

experience in health services but no previous formal medical education.[25] The Health Manpower Act of 1971 included funding for physician assistant training, and by 1974 the number of existing educational training programs had doubled.

With the assistance of these programs of the 1960s and 1970s, not only did the health status of U.S. citizens improve, but, at the same time, real results were seen in the increased enrollment of more minority students in medical schools.[26] Some believed that the problems of access to care and distribution of health manpower were solved. Others believed that the changing health care environment and rising health care costs of the 1980s forced these issues to be tabled. Certainly the GMENAC report predicting an oversupply of physicians by 1990 shifted the focus from the need to educate medical personnel to ways of curtailing health care expenditures.

The combination of cuts in funding of programs that have helped to educate minority students for the health professions and a disavowal of affirmative action policies is creating a diminution of opportunities for minorities that may once again be redressed by public action. The need for such action is beginning to be heard in public forums and in the literature.[27-29] It is timely to examine trends of minority practice in the physician assistant profession and determine what steps are appropriate to ensure continued, adequate minority representation.

Respondents who identified themselves as members of a racial minority in the 1984 Masterfile Survey showed that changes are occurring in the racial composition of the profession. The nonrespondent survey indicated that the study findings accurately reflect the proportion of minority physician assistants in practice, however. Table 3-1 shows the number and percentage of respondents to the three most recent physician assistant surveys by their self-reported racial identity.

Table 3-1 Respondents to Physician Assistant Surveys by Race/Ethnicity

Race/Ethnicity	1978		1981		1984	
	Number	Percent	Number	Percent	Number	Percent
White	3,925	87.7	5,513	91.4	5,784	91.39
Black	234	5.2	196	3.3	188	2.97
Hispanic	109	2.4	122	2.0	173	2.73
Oriental	43	1.0	69	1.1	NA	NA
Native American	66	1.5	76	1.3	NA	NA
None of the above	94	2.2	53	.9	NA	NA
Other	NA	NA	NA	NA	184	2.91
TOTAL	4,471	100.00	6,029	100.00	6,329	100.00

Sources: National Physician Assistant Survey, Association of Physician Assistant Programs, May 1982; *1984 Masterfile Survey,* American Academy of Physician Assistants, 1984.

Table 3-1 indicates that participation by blacks either in the profession itself, or in survey response, has dropped in both actual numbers and as a proportion of the total population of physician assistants. Participation by other minorities has dropped in the same time period, except for Hispanics who appear to have better representation in 1984 than in 1978.

Enrollment figures for physician assistant programs in the 1983–1984 and 1985–1986 classes indicate a higher proportion of minority participation than in the profession as a whole[30,31] (Table 3-2). The discrepancy between the survey figures and the enrollment figures may be attributed to the attrition rate before graduation and from the profession itself. Statistics assembled by the Association of Physician Assistant Programs (APAP) show an overall estimated attrition rate in 1985 of 11.5 percent, but 23.3 percent for black students from physician assistant educational programs.

Variables from the Masterfile Survey were analyzed using SAS ANOVA procedures. A simple examination of the data indicates that the following variables differed between minority and nonminority respondents at the $P < .01$ level of significance. (Practice setting and specialty had such few numbers that validity of the significance test for these variables is called into question.)

- practice setting
- specialty
- patient income
- patient age
- patient race
- hours on call

Table 3-2 Enrollment for Physician Assistant Students by Race/Ethnicity

Race/Ethnicity	1983–1984 (Second-year students) Mean Number Enrolled per Program	Percent	1985–1986 Mean Number Enrolled per Program	Percent
White/Non-Hispanic	20.7	86	20.9	85.3
Black/Non-Hispanic	1.6	7	1.8	7.3
Hispanic	1.1	5	1.1	4.5
American Indian/Alaskan	.1	< 1	NA	NA
Asian/Pacific Islander	.3	< 1	NA	NA
Other	.2	< 1	.7	2.9

Sources: First and Second Annual Reports on Physician Assistant Educational Programs in the United States, 1984–1985, 1985–1986, Association of Physician Assistant Programs, © 1985, 1986.

- hours in office
- hours in hospital ward
- hours in delivery room
- hours providing patient care
- hours performing administrative tasks

Salary levels for physician assistants do not differ between minority and nonminority practitioners (Table 3-3). This fact is encouraging and is one indication that the profession is a very good one for minorities to enter.

Minority physician assistants are seeing a somewhat different patient population than their nonminority peers. In every measure, minority physician assistants see poorer and younger patients who are more likely to be of the same ethnic group than patients seen by other practitioners (Tables 3-4 and 3-5).

Minority and nonminority physician assistants practice in different specialties and settings as well. Minorities are well represented in general practice, family practice, internal medicine, pediatrics, psychiatry, public health, and general surgery. However, twice as many nonminorities are found in surgical specialties than minorities. The practice setting varies among all the minority groups identified in the survey. Blacks are disproportionately found serving in federal hospitals, state hospitals, city hospitals, private hospitals, community clinics, nursing homes, military hospitals, clinics, and federal and city prisons.

Population projections indicate a growing demand for health care among minority groups in the United States. The U.S. Bureau of the Census projections indicate that compared to 1980, when 12 percent of the population 65 years or older was nonwhite, by the year 2050, 18 percent of the older population of the United States will be nonwhite.[32] The fastest growing segment of the population is the minority elderly, and their need for health services will be greater than the rest of the younger minority population, as well as their nonminority peers.[33]

In 1985 it was found that 56 percent of patient visits to black physicians were from black patients and 77 percent of patient visits to white physicians were by

Table 3-3 Physician Assistant Income (Mean) by Race/Ethnicity

Race/Ethnicity	Number	Salary (Dollars)
Black	183	27,240
Hispanic	163	29,616
Other	169	28,328
White	5,505	27,458

Source: 1984 Masterfile Survey, American Academy of Physician Assistants, © 1984.

Table 3-4 Patient Income and Age by Race/Ethnicity of Physician Assistant

Physician Assistant Race/Ethnicity	Patient Income (Dollars)	Patient Age (Mean)
Black	13,652	40.5
Hispanic	17,025	37.1
Other	15,671	37.6
White	20,162	41.3

Source: 1984 Masterfile Survey, American Academy of Physician Assistants, © 1984.

whites.[34] One can infer from this finding that the training of more minority health professionals increases access for minorities. From the Masterfile Survey of physician assistants, it would appear that it also increases access for the poor and the institutionalized.

Educational programs that train health care personnel must be concerned about the representativeness of their applicant pool, their enrollees, and their graduates if they intend to contribute to the representative distribution of health care throughout the nation. The physician assistant profession shows this concern, as evidenced by increasing enrollment of minority students in its programs and the careful attention to recording data on their applications, acceptance, and graduation. It is noteworthy, however, that 41 percent of the physician assistant training programs reported in a recent survey that they had no black students enrolled in either their 1984–85 or 1985–86 classes.[35]

Orque, Block, and Monrroy list several deterrents to the participation of ethnic minorities in the nursing profession.[36] These may be applicable to physician assistants as well:

Table 3-5 Physician Assistant Race/Ethnicity by Patient Race/Ethnicity

Patient Race/Ethnicity	Physician Assistant Race/Ethnicity			
	Black	Hispanic	White	Other
Black	44.2	16.5	19.9	20.2
Hispanic	17.9	34.1	9.5	15.4
White	34.0	44.3	65.8	38.4
Other	3.3	4.6	4.2	25.6
None	0.6	0.5	0.6	0.4

Source: 1984 Masterfile Survey, American Academy of Physician Assistants, © 1984.

- inadequate role models
- deficiencies in educational preparation and counseling
- lack of motivation, confidence, and peer group support
- need for financial aid
- lack of faculty and administrative commitment

Many programs have taken steps to overcome these deterrents and have spent both energy and resources to demonstrate a commitment to making their programs representative of the population that they serve.[37] The following suggestions have already been put into effect in some programs in part or in full. They serve as a reminder to others that a climate of successful recruitment, retention, and graduation can be built into every program.

- Foster an awareness of the heterogeneity of student backgrounds and needs.
- Provide academic help before and during the program.
- Hire a representative staff that reflects the ethnicity of the population to be served.
- Expend the effort needed to develop clerkships with minority physicians and in health care institutions serving large numbers of minority patients.
- Include material in the curriculum that develops cultural sensitivity and includes the participation of the minority community and their health providers.
- Include minority students in the decision making about how the program will be structured.
- Encourage interaction among minority and nonminority students and faculty.
- Request input from minority students on recruitment programs.
- Maintain a listing of financial aid resources available to the program students, and counsel minority students regarding these resources.
- Seek linkages with the minority affairs committees of the associations of physician assistants for role model enhancement.
- Develop self-paced audiovisual aids.
- Conduct inservice training with the faculty regarding facilitating minority success in the program.
- Form an advisory group on minority recruitment and retention composed of both students and faculty.

In addition to the steps that can be taken by the educational programs that train physician assistants, in 1986 the AAPA began an effort to recruit students from minority communities at an early stage in their career decision making. Called

Project Access, this initiative will develop educational materials to explain the profession to youngsters and encourage their development of skills and interests that would make them viable candidates for physician assistant programs.

By following trends of minority involvement in all aspects of the profession and making efforts to increase representation and opportunities for minorities, the interests of physician assistants are best served. Certainly, minorities must have access to practice in every environment and setting and with all patients, regardless of race and ethnicity. Their presence in the profession ensures an awareness of issues central to health care concerns of the community and increases the likelihood of fulfilling the first physician assistant charge: bringing health care to all parts of the community.

CONCLUSION

Physician assistants are well represented among the health care providers who are serving the underserved. More than 12 percent are working in public hospitals, another 6 percent are in community health clinics, and almost 4 percent work in prisons. Many work after hours to provide volunteer services to the very poor and the homeless. Some are working overseas in refugee camps or in Third World countries.

It is important that physician assistants work with the proper supervision and concern on the part of the medical team. It is vital that they are not perceived as providing second class service or contributing to a multi-tiered system of health care. This can be avoided by responsible assessment of ways in which health care can be provided and helping keep other members of the system accountable for decisions that affect the welfare of those who need low-cost, quality care.

NOTES

1. *1984 Masterfile Survey* (Arlington, VA: American Academy of Physician Assistants, 1984).

2. US Dept of Health and Human Services. *GMENAC: Report to the Secretary of Health and Human Services.* 1980. US Dept of Health and Human Services.

3. Karen Davis and Cathy Schoen, *Health and the War on Poverty* (Washington, DC: Brookings Institute, 1978), pp. 41–48.

4. Drew Altman, "Health Care for the Poor," *Annals, AAPSS* 468(1983):103–123 (p. 111).

5. Robert J. Blendon, et al., "Uncompensated Care by Hospitals or Public Insurance for the Poor: Does it Make a Difference?" *The New England Journal of Medicine* 314(1986):1160.

6. Donald O. Nutter, "Access to Care and the Evolution of Corporate, For-Profit Medicine," *New England Journal of Medicine* 311(1984):917–919.

7. M. Harvey Brenner, "Estimating the Effects of Economic Change on National Well-Being," Subcommittee on Economic Goals and Intergovernmental Policy, Joint Economic Committee of Congress (Washington, DC: Government Printing Office, 1984).

8. Alan C. Monheit, et al., "The Employed Uninsured and the Role of Public Policy," *Inquiry* 22(1985):348–364.

9. Donald R. Cohodes, "America: The Home of the Free, the Land of the Uninsured," *Inquiry* 23(1986):228.

10. US Dept of Health and Human Services, National Institute of Mental Health. "Role of Nurses in Meeting the Health/Mental Health Needs of the Homeless" (Proceedings of a Workshop, Washington, DC, 6–7 May 1986).

11. James B. Reuler, et al., "Physician House Call Services for the Medically Needy Inner City Residents," *American Journal of Public Health* 76(1986):1131–1134.

12. Mary O'Neil Mundinger, "Health Service Funding Cuts and the Declining Health of the Poor," *New England Journal of Medicine* 313(1985):45.

13. Children's Defense Fund, *Black and White Children in America* (Washington, DC: Children's Defense Fund, 1985).

14. *Report of the Secretary's Task Force on Black and Minority Health*. 1985. US Dept of Health and Human Services, p. 21.

15. Ibid., p. 211.

16. *Data on Earned Degrees Conferred by Institutions or Higher Education by Race, Ethnicity and Sex Academic Year 1976–1977*. 1979. US Dept of Health, Education, and Welfare, Office of Civil Rights.

17. Albert P. Williams et al., *Factors Affecting Medical School Admissions Decisions for Minority Applicants: A Comparative Study of Ten Schools* (Santa Monica, CA: Rand Corporation, 1979).

18. Wilbertine P. Philpot and Stuart Bernstein, *Minorities and Women in the Health Fields: Applicants, Students, and Workers*. US Dept of Health, Education, and Welfare, 1978.

19. William Cadbury and Charlotte M. Cadbury. *Medical Education Responses to a Challenge: Minorities and the Disadvantaged, Development and Representation in the Health Professions* (Mount Kisco, NY: Futura Publishing Co., 1979).

20. Leonard S. Baker and Norma Gill. *Minority Medical Students: Who They Are, Their Progress, Career Aspiration, Their Future in Medical Schools*. 1978. US Dept of Health, Education, and Welfare.

21. Stephen N. Keith et al. "Effects of Affirmative Action in Medical Schools: A Study of the Class of 1975," *New England Journal of Medicine* 313(1985):1519–1541.

22. Sylvia Drew Ivey, "Ending Discrimination in Health Care: A Dream Deferred" (Speech presented at U.S. Civil Rights Commission Hearings, Washington, D.C., 15 April 1980).

23. Karen Davis and Cathy Schoen. *Health and the War on Poverty* (Washington, DC: Brookings Institute, 1978).

24. B. Phillips, et al, "Minority Recruitment to the Health Professions: A Matched Comparison Six-Year Follow-up," *Journal of Medical Education* 56(1981):742–747.

25. E.S. Schneller, *The Physician Assistant: Innovation in the Medical Division of Labor* (Lexington, MA: Lexington Books, 1978), p. xx.

26. Steven Shea and M.T. Fullilove, "Entry of Blacks and Other Minorities into U.S. Medical Schools," *New England Journal of Medicine* 313(October 10, 1985):933–940.

27. Ibid., p. 939.

28. John Inglehart, "Federal Support of Health Manpower," *New England Journal of Medicine* 314 (January 30, 1986):324–328.

29. "Improved Care for Black Patients Stressed by NMA," *American Medical News*, January 10, 1986, p. 23.

30. Denis Oliver. *First Annual Report on Physician Assistant Educational Programs in the United States, 1984–85* (Arlington, VA: Association of Physician Assistant Programs, 1985), p. 24.

31. Denis Oliver. *Second Annual Report on Physician Assistant Educational Programs in the United States, 1985–1986.* (Arlington, VA: Association of Physician Assistant Programs, 1986), p. 26.

32. US Senate Special Committee on Aging, in conjunction with the American Association of Retired Persons, *Aging America: Trends and Projections* (Washington, DC: US Government Printing Office, PL3377C(584), 1984), p. 10.

33. *Characteristics of the Black Elderly 1980.* 1980. US Dept of Health, Education, and Welfare, Pub. No. 80-20057, p. 19.

34. S.N. Keith et al., *op cit.,* p. 1522.

35. Denis Oliver, *Second Annual Report on Physician Assistant Educational Programs in the United States, 1985–86, op. cit.,* p. 26.

36. Modesta Soberano Orque, Bobbie Block, and Lidia Monrroy, *Ethnic Nursing Care: A Multicultural Approach* (St. Louis, C.V. Mosby, 1983).

37. Jack Liskin, "A Model Project for Recruitment and Education of Disadvantaged Students in a Physician Assistant Program" (Proceedings of the Association of Physician Assistant Programs Paper Presentations. San Antonio, TX, May, 1985), pp. 12-24.

Chapter 4

The Cost Effectiveness of Physician Assistants

Ken Harbert is a physician assistant who is an administrator at one of the largest tertiary care centers in the country. In this interview, he discusses the role that the physician assistant can play in limiting the costs of health care.

Gretchen Schafft: I want to talk to you about cost effectiveness. What have you discovered about the cost effectiveness of physician assistants?

Ken Harbert: Physician services augmented by physician assistant services in the community are cost effective because physician assistants will provide at least three to four times the amount of revenue and services that they receive in income and benefits. In other words, their clinical services far exceed their costs to the health care institution. A physician can utilize two physician assistants and double, or in some cases even more than double, the services he or she can provide. This means that the physician does not have to see every patient, although the physician may choose to see every patient under some circumstances. For some of the services that the physician assistant provides, the physician does not necessarily have to be there physically.

The key, really, to cost effectiveness is the efficiency in which you use the physician or the physician assistant in specific styles of practice. We think the physician is more efficient in providing one type of service and the physician assistant more efficient in another. For instance, we think physician assistants are more effective in providing personal follow-up care because they allow patients time to discuss their problems, receive feedback, and feel better about the services that have been provided.

The patient population must be happy with the care they receive or you won't remain the source of their care. These visits, of course, are what generate revenue for the institution. In follow-up care, we are also very interested in using the staff efficiently. A physician assistant can do a follow-up visit much more effectively and efficiently than other health care providers in most cases.

Gretchen Schafft: To what extent can a physician assistant make a contribution to cost-effective health care? How much of the cost effectiveness is in the purview of the physician assistant, and how much of it is outside of this realm of influence?

Ken Harbert: That is a very good question. It depends to a large extent on the relationship of the physician assistant to the physician. In private practice where there is a one-on-one relationship with the physician, it is very easy for the physician assistant to have some control of his or her efficiency if the relationship with the physician is good. I say that because if it's a good one-on-one relationship, it's easy for the physician assistant to say, "These are things that I can see and that I enjoy seeing and that I can see in mass volume. But these are things that are going to take me longer and that probably you would be better suited to see." So there is communication, cooperation, and coordination that allow the physician assistant to be very useful to that physician.

Now that works also in a group setting, but in any kind of group dynamic situation, the more people involved, the more difficult it becomes to keep those lines of communication, those lines of cooperation, clear. And the more individuals who are involved in that kind of decision making, the more difficult the communication becomes. A physician assistant working for two physicians, each with his or her own separate style of practice, is going to have to adapt to each of these styles of practice. It becomes difficult for the physician assistant to focus in on each style of practice. The individual physician's needs, skills, and ways of seeing patients will be unique, because no two physicians will see medical practice the same way.

Gretchen Schafft: Are there trade-offs, do you think, when people become very concerned about cost effectiveness? Do you think there are trade-offs in patient care?

Ken Harbert: That's the DRG question-of-the-year, isn't it? The question is whether DRGs are making the quality of care better or worse. It becomes almost a philosophical issue about the practice of medicine. Who makes the decisions as to what's important and what is not important? Do I say, for example, that we aren't going to deliver any more babies because our insurance rates are going to be too high? Do we look at the outliers of DRGs and say we don't want to deal with those kinds of patients? Do we say that this is a DRG category that gets the highest amount of revenue and that's the only service we want to provide and we want to provide even more services for those individuals? Do we want to open up a new center outside the hospital because we know that that center will generate more revenue than if it is kept within the hospital, even though it has already been functioning very very well for 10 or 15 years within the hospital? Do we want to come up with a new style of doing an operation, for example, because it is more cost effective?

Maybe we ought to look at the other side of that question: Can you say that, if physicians practice more cost effectively, they are also going to be providing a better quality of care? Are they going to look at serious problems and minor problems and treat each differently? Maybe that's the good side of cost-effective management. I think we all need to be very wise about how we provide our services, how the consumer feels about the services we provide, and continue to demand quality of care. I believe that costs can be lowered by the competent, prudent health professional who continues to practice by "doing no harm" both personally and financially to the patient.

THE COST EFFECTIVENESS OF PHYSICIAN ASSISTANTS

The performance of physician assistants in the delivery of medical care services has been extensively evaluated over the 20-year history of the profession. Spitzer notes that the introduction of physician assistants has been a "responsible policy" and states that "many other innovations mediated by medical practitioners have gained widespread acceptance with much less rigorous prior evaluation than was given to . . . physician assistants."[1] The impact of physician assistants on access to health care services, quality of care, and physician and patient acceptance has been thoroughly measured with positive results. Less clear is the precise degree of physician assistant productivity in clinical practice and, by extension, the cost effectiveness of the utilization of these professionals.

This chapter examines the issue of physician assistant cost effectiveness and the financial impact of utilizing physician assistants in clinical practice. The major studies that have examined physician assistant productivity and cost effectiveness and the limitations and generalizability of this data are considered. The chapter also assesses the applicability of cost-effectiveness analysis (CEA) to physician assistant health manpower and, by inference, the difficulties in making determinations of cost effectiveness in circumstances involving such a complex activity as the content of medical work. Finally, the beneficiaries of physician assistant cost effectiveness are considered. That is, if physician assistants are indeed cost effective, do the benefits of physician assistant utilization accrue to the employer, the patient, or society as a whole?

The question of physician assistant cost effectiveness is relevant from a number of perspectives. For some years, a number of federal health policy organizations have attempted to assess physician assistant cost effectiveness, particularly in relation to the government's investment in physician assistant education and deployment. Such groups have included the Congressional Budget Office, the Congressional Office of Technology Assessment, the Health Care Finance Administration, and the Bureau of Health Professions. These groups have also considered the issue of physician assistant cost effectiveness from the perspective of cost savings when practices employing physician assistants are reimbursed through Medicare. The 1986 passage of a bill providing Medicare coverage to physician assistants in selected settings suggests that policy makers recognize the capabilities of physician assistants in providing quality care at a reasonable cost. Demonstration of physician assistant cost effectiveness could have a significant and positive effect on the hiring and utilization of these professionals, not only by private fee-for-service practitioners but also by hospitals, long-term care facilities, prepaid groups, and other health delivery systems. In the present climate of cost containment in health care, considerations of more efficient and economic delivery of medical care have become vitally important. Knowledge that the utilization of physician assistants is cost effective could lead to further measures that would limit the increase in expenditures for medical care.

LIMITATIONS OF COST-EFFECTIVENESS ANALYSIS

Cost-effectiveness analysis is a relatively new technique designed to compare the positive and negative consequences of a specific resource allocation.[2] It seeks to measure the comparable benefit of a particular investment versus its cost. In health care this technique is commonly applied to new medical technologies, diagnostic and laboratory tests, health facilities and delivery systems, and drug treatment and immunization programs. In a number of cases, it is possible to compare directly the benefits and cost of a specific intervention because both the investment and the outcome can be measured in monetary terms; for example, the introduction of a new antibiotic. In other instances, the outcome cannot be assigned a monetary value and must be expressed in terms of years of life saved, days of morbidity avoided, and so forth. Additionally, comparisons involving monetary and nonmonetary factors usually end up posing a complex value judgment, e.g., "Is a cost of $50,000 per person per year of life saved acceptable?" The answers to such questions go beyond mere financial considerations and thus fall into the domain of social and public health policy.

The application of cost-effectiveness analysis in general to the delivery of medical care services and specifically to the provider of such services is also a complex endeavor. It is difficult to measure accurately the content of a medical encounter, given variations in such factors as severity of illness, types of treatment, patient preferences, extent of use of diagnostic tests, level of provider training, and the site and mode of care delivery. Add to these factors the differences in the type of provider delivering a similar service, different systems of provider reimbursement and payment, as well as different styles of task delegation, and it becomes obvious that any efforts seeking to determine cost effectiveness tend to be methodologically difficult and quite expensive.

When one considers the use of physician assistants as the intervention in a cost-effectiveness analysis, further methodological difficulties arise. Physician assistants provide medical care services that to a large extent overlap with those services provided by physicians. Although most studies suggest that physician assistants can perform anywhere from 50 to 75 percent of the services performed by doctors,[3] it is not clear which services are included in these percentages and which are left out. These percentages may also vary depending on practice setting and specialty. A major variable is also the degree of delegation of tasks by an individual physician to a physician assistant. It is known that degrees of delegation vary among different types of physician specialists and among physicians in private practice versus those in other settings.[4]

Most studies that have attempted to look specifically at physician assistant cost effectiveness suffer from flaws based on the above-described constraints. They generally have small sample sizes, analyze only experiences in the ambulatory setting, include types of health practitioners who may or may not be comparable to physician assistants (i.e., nurses, nurse practitioners), focus only on primary care functions, and are incomplete with regard to revenue generation and cost data. Further, the majority of these studies were performed in the early to mid-1970s when the role of the physician assistant was still developing.

Bearing in mind these limitations and recognizing that the published data are suggestive but not conclusive, it is asserted that the cost effectiveness of physician assistants can be reasonably confirmed, if not precisely measured, by the data. Major studies of physician assistant productivity and cost effectiveness have shown that physician assistants usually generate practice revenue far beyond the costs of their salaries and overhead. In addition, an important factor not commonly emphasized in major reviews is the nonmonetary contribution made by physician assistants to medical practice—a factor even more difficult to quantify than cost effectiveness. Lastly, even though one may never be able to precisely measure physician assistant cost effectiveness in every practice setting and specialty, the fact that over 18,000 physician assistants are currently employed is significant empirical evidence for cost effectiveness. Employers—physicians, clinics, hospitals—would not hire physician assistants were they not to some degree cost effective.

REVIEW OF THE LITERATURE

From the bulk of published studies evaluating physician assistant performance it is clear that the majority of medical care tasks traditionally provided by physicians can be performed by physician assistants. Anywhere from 60 to 80 percent of the tasks performed by primary care physicians can be provided by physician assistants without consultation.[4,5] Extensive studies show that the substitution ratio of physician assistants to physicians falls in the range of .50 to .75, suggesting that it would take one physician assistant to substitute for one-half to three-quarters of a physician.[4] Other studies confirm that the clinical productivity of physician assistants in primary care falls within this range.[6,7]

If we accept the fact that physician assistants are one-half to three-quarters as productive as physicians and if we recognize that the mean salary of a physician assistant in 1984 was $24,500[8] compared with a mean salary for licensed physicians of $106,300 in that same year,[9] we can begin to appreciate the considerable cost effectiveness of physician assistants in clinical practice.

Almost all of the studies of physician assistant productivity utilize one of three approaches: (1) comparisons of the amount of time taken by physicians and physician assistants to complete an office visit, (2) comparisons of the number of visits handled by different types of providers in a given period of time, and (3) assessments of the effect of adding a physician assistant on the total number of patient visits. Most studies show that physician assistants spend more time per patient during office visits than physicians.[10] In one national survey physician assistants averaged 14.2 direct patient encounters per day, 2.6 telephone encounters per day, and spent 13.3 minutes per encounter, compared with supervising physicians who averaged 18.9 direct patient encounters per day, 3.4 telephone encounters per day, and spent 11 minutes per encounter.[7] Other recent productivity data reveal that, in selected rural health delivery organizations, primary care physicians see an average of 105.6 patients per week and work 48.6 hours per week, whereas physician assistants see an average of 75 patients per week and work 40.7 hours per week.[11] These data suggest that physician assistants are productive to the practices that employ them and tend to confirm the aforementioned substitutability ratio of .50 to .75. Thus, physician assistants offer the advantage of being nearly three-quarters as productive as physicians, yet their overall employment cost is far less than that of physicians. The final report of the Physician Extender Reimbursement Study stated:

> Practices with physician extenders (PAs or NPs) provide more patient visits per $1,000 of practice cost, at a higher quality of care, and with less charge to the patient or third party payer than do traditional practices. The use of physician assistants in ambulatory care settings appears to be beneficial in terms of costs, providers, and patients.[12]

Ott at the University of Colorado conducted a carefully designed study of the financial impact of physician assistants on fee-for-service pediatric practices.[5] Nine practices were prospectively examined before, during, and after the addition of a child health associate. Detailed financial records for 12 months before and after the child health associates (CHAs) were employed in these practices were obtained and analyzed. The child health associates saw 14 patients a day while the total number of patients seen in the practice was increased by 10 per day. The total number of office visits increased an average of 28 percent. During the first 12 months of employment, CHAs generated an average of $37,807 in fees-for-services provided. On the average, the CHAs derived 67 percent of this revenue from office visits, 4 percent from procedures, 13 percent from immunizations, 15 percent from laboratory tests, and 1 percent from miscellaneous charges. The average total practice income increased $33,318 over the control year. Of that amount $28,944 was accounted for by the increased number of patients seen. As a percentage, the total income of the practices increased 27 percent. The average cost of employment of the CHA (wages, fringe benefits, overhead) was $18,800. The investigators calculated that the breakeven point was reached if the CHA saw only eight patients per day. Because in fact they saw nearly double that number, all the CHAs were paying their own way by the end of the first year and some by the end of their first month in practice.[5]

An overall examination of physician assistant productivity and cost effectiveness was included in a report of the congressional Office of Technology Assessment. This document analyzed physician assistants and nurse practitioners from the point of view of cost savings to society generated by the utilization of these practitioners. It contained an extensive review of the literature on physician assistant and nurse practitioner cost effectiveness and admitted that the existing data preclude a definitive cost-effectiveness analysis. Nonetheless, the report states that "on the basis of available data, it appears that physician assistants do alter the production of medical services in a manner that can improve access to such services and reduce production costs" and further concludes that "the use of physician assistants results in productivity gains and cost reductions."[13] The report notes that the financial benefits derived from the cost effectiveness of physician assistants (or nurse practitioners) accrue primarily to the physician or employing institution, but emphasizes that when physician assistants (or nurse practitioners) are used in a prepaid group practice setting, such as an HMO, the economic gains of using these practitioners may serve to keep overall patient premium costs down. As another observer states, "HMOs have strong incentives to contain costs, and their structure and size provide the opportunity to capitalize upon the economies of scale and the division of labor that the utilization of physician assistants can offer."[4]

In summary, the literature reveals that physician assistants are clinically productive at a rate (in primary care) of about one-half to three-quarters that of physicians. Given that physician assistant salary costs are about one-fifth to one-fourth that of physicians, it seems clear that physician assistants are cost effective to their employing practices. The research data show that physician assistants perform at these rates of clinical productivity in a manner in which quality of care is maintained at high levels[14] and that patient acceptance and physician acceptance are strongly positive.[10] The best data showing physician assistant cost effectiveness emanate from studies done in an HMO setting,[3] and these data appear, but not conclusively, to be able to be generalized to other patient care settings.

FROM THE DATA TO THE REAL WORLD

In considering the question of physician assistant cost effectiveness in the late 1980s, we must recognize several broad considerations not extensively discussed in the literature review of the existing information and its application to the current status of physician assistant utilization in clinical practice.

- The existing data pertain only to primary care practice; more than 40 percent of physician assistants in 1986 worked in specialty practice.[15]
- Even in primary care, the .50 to .75 figure of physician assistant substitutability may vary from primary care practice to primary care practice; the content of tasks included in these figures may differ.
- Over 30 percent of physician assistants now work in hospital settings where their duties may include a significant amount of technical procedures, particularly in subspecialties, such as cardiothoracic surgery, neonatology, and invasive cardiology; under these circumstances, it is difficult to analyze accurately the degree of physician assistant productivity and consequently their cost effectiveness.
- The existing variations in state medical practice acts for physician assistants, physician assistant prescribing laws and patterns, and third party reimbursement policies have a marked effect on physician assistant practice and productivity;[16,17] these variations are not accounted for in the data.
- A number of physician assistants seem to be involved in the delivery of physician-complementary services, such as patient education and preventive services; we do not yet know the extent to which physician assistants are used in these types of roles nor how cost beneficial they are in these practices. The fact that preventive services are not usually reimbursed by third party payers hampers the potential of physician assistants to provide these services to employing practices.

It should be fairly obvious, therefore, that physician assistant practice today is tremendously variable across setting and specialty lines. The utilization of physician assistants is no longer confined to primary care in private offices but is dispersed across the spectrum of medical care delivery.[18] Consequently, it becomes exceedingly difficult to measure the physician assistant input into a given practice or hospital service.

Given the inadequacies and abstractness of the existing health services research data on physician assistant cost effectiveness, the question then becomes: Is it possible to assess or infer physician assistant cost effectiveness from the known current capacities and patterns of physician assistant utilization? The answer involves not only the monetary benefits of using physician assistants but also noneconomic considerations.

Economic Benefits of Physician Assistant Utilization

In order to demonstrate physician assistant cost effectiveness in a meaningful way, it is necessary to consider the effects of physician assistant utilization across specialty and setting lines. In view of these important variables, data on physician assistant cost effectiveness were considered from four perspectives: physician assistants in office-based primary care practice, physician assistants in an organized health delivery system, physician assistants in a corporate medical system, and physician assistants as inpatient specialty providers in large medical centers.

Private Practice

Carter examined data from a 1981 national survey of 6,056 practicing physician assistants.[8] From the data reported by physician assistants, it was possible to determine the number of office visits performed by them in three specialties—family practice, internal medicine, and pediatrics—the mean fee charged to patients for the visit, and their average salaries. These data are presented in Table 4-1. It can be seen that physician assistants generate considerable revenue for employing practices that is substantially greater than the mean salaries of these providers and substantially greater than the total expenses (salary, fringe benefits, and cost of physician supervision) incurred by their employment.

Table 4-1 Mean Productivity, Practice Revenue, Annual Salary of Physician Assistants' Office-Based Specialties

	Family Medicine	Internal Medicine	Pediatrics
Patients seen per year by physician assistant	5206	4558	4743
Average fee per patient	$18.86	$29.12	$19.68
Revenue generated	$98,185	$132,728	$93,365
Physician assistant salary	$22,400	$22,100	$20,200
Total physician assistant[a] expenses	$35,190	$36,185	$32,570
Mean net income[b] of physician in specialty	$71,900	$85,600	$73,200
Cost benefit[c]	$62,995	$96,543	$60,795

[a]Includes salary, 25% fringes and overhead, and 10% of physician time for supervision.
[b]Figures (1982) taken from Crozier and Iglehart.[9]
[c]Derived from this formula: physician assistant revenue generated minus total physician assistant expenses.

Source: Unless noted, this table is adapted from *Secondary Analysis: The 1981 National Survey of Physician Assistants* by R.D. Carter et al., with permission of Association of Physician Assistant Programs, © June 1984.

Thus, if physician assistant cost effectiveness is measured in strictly economic terms (total revenue generated by physician assistant minus total physician assistant expenses), it becomes clear by any definition that the employment of a physician assistant in an office-based setting results in substantial revenue gain for that practice. It would also seem reasonable that this data could be generalizable to include both solo and group private practices, the practice setting for over 35 percent of all practicing physician assistants. Data gathered by the AMA on the impact of employing a physician assistant or nurse practitioner in private practice in 1982 also suggest a favorable cost-effectiveness picture, in that practices employing such providers saw more patients and increased the net income of the physician (Table 4-2).[19]

Organized Health Systems/HMOs

It is in organized health delivery systems that physician assistants are known to be particularly cost effective. As one study states,

> Organized settings that operate on fixed budgets (prepaid group practices, certain clinics, corporations) have a much greater incentive to employ . . . physician assistants. It is to their financial advantage to produce services with the most efficient combination of inputs, sub-

Table 4-2 Impact of Employment of a Physician Assistant or Nurse Practitioner in Private Practice, 1981

Practice Characteristics	Private Practice without Physician Assistant/Nurse Practitioner	Private Practice with Physician Assistant/Nurse Practitioner
Patient visits per hour[a]	3.2	3.9
Patient visits per week[a]	86.2	103.1
Physicians' weeks worked per year	46.6	46.7
Physicians' net income[a] ($000)	93.7	106.0
Fee—office visit for established patient	$23.19	$22.45

[a]Differences in values are significant at the 1% level.

Source: Adapted from *SMS Report*, Vol. 1, No. 10, with permission of American Medical Association, © December 1982.

stituting lower priced physician extenders for higher priced physicians whenever possible.[13]

From the experience with physician assistants of the Kaiser-Permanente Health Plan in Portland it was determined that one physician assistant can substitute for 63 percent of a physician at 38 percent of the physician's cost.[3] Greenfield et al. reported on the effects of an experimental physician assistant protocol system introduced at the Southern California Kaiser-Permanente Facility.[20] They found that, before the study, ten physicians and three physician extenders saw 2,700 patients per month; two years after the study, six and one-half FTE physicians and six physician extenders saw 2,900 patients per month. The authors concluded that the use of physician assistants in this protocol system resulted in a 20 percent reduction in average visit costs. Whether this savings could or should reduce costs to patients is a related health policy issue.

Corporate Medical Systems

There are also data from the corporate sector that speak to the cost effectiveness of midlevel practitioners (physician assistants and nurse practitioners). It is generally assumed that, for the purposes of productivity and clinical capabilities, physician assistants and nurse practitioners are basically interchangeable.[10] Many studies of cost effectiveness, quality of care, and reproductivity considered both types of midlevel practitioners and regard them as equivalent.[21]

A report from the corporate medical services division of Tennaco, Inc. of Houston describes how the use of four nurse practitioners employed as primary care providers results in significant cost savings.[22] Using data that compared the costs of providing health services to its employees by relying on community (fee-for-service) resources with the costs of providing the same types of services in-house (using nurse practitioners with physician backup), Tennaco found that the in-house system was significantly less expensive. For an employee population of 14,374 using 19,963 services (visits), the cost of providing health care using community resources was estimated to be (market value) $978,057 in 1983. The total cost of the in-house provider system in 1983 was $469,562 (Table 4-3). Thus, Tennaco was able to provide health services to its employees using nurse practitioners at about one-half of the costs of using community providers for the same care. The authors suggest that "industry should examine more closely the nurse practitioner as a cost-effective health care provider."[22]

Hospitals

The fastest-growing area of physician assistant employment is the hospital setting. Physician assistants are increasingly employed on surgical, medical, and pediatric services as junior housestaff providing a wide range of inpatient services.

Table 4-3 Cost Comparison Study of Physician Extenders in Tennaco, Inc.

Health Services Provided	Market Value ($)	Health Services Expenditures	Costs ($)
Occupation-related service	109,805	Health services budget	260,128
Non-occupation-related service	462,491	(physician extender salaries,	
X-ray	5,883	overhead)	
Laboratory	188,028	Physician salaries	74,000
Screening tests and special		Laboratory fees	3,015
procedures	211,850	Spare rental	132,419
Total	978,057	Total	469,562

Source: Adapted from *Business & Health*, pp. 26–27, with permission of Washington Business Group on Health, © September 1984.

Physician assistants also work with hospital-based specialists and subspecialists; their duties include not only routine patient care but also involvement in clinical research, utilization in special units, such as burn services and critical care areas, and the performance of special diagnostic and therapeutic procedures, e.g., endoscopy, colonoscopy, and coronary angiography. In all cases, the level of function of the physician assistant is comparable to that of a first-year resident.[23] In many of these hospitals, physician assistants have replaced full-time licensed physician house officers whose salaries would be double or even triple the salaries paid to physician assistants. In other instances, physician assistants assume the duties performed by residents and fellows, and although their salaries are roughly equivalent ($25,000–$30,000 per year), they offer a number of other important advantages, as described below.

Frick from the Detroit Medical Center/Wayne State University has carefully documented the experience of shifting to a physician assistant-augmented house-staff in a large internal medicine residency program.[24] In 1978 several physician assistants were hired for the oncology division of Harper-Grace Hospitals, a major division of the Detroit Medical Center. At that time the division needed to provide increased patient care service as a result of changes in the oncology fellowship curriculum. The experience with the oncology division allowed the institution to assess the capacities of physician assistants on inpatient services and led to the expanded use of physician assistants by other sections in the department of medicine. By 1986, 32 physician assistants were working in the department covering 396 beds on inpatient wards in three hospitals of the medical center. The internal medicine residency program was modified to incorporate the use of physician assistants. Physician assistants provided a number of important benefits to the institution, including improvement of patient care, enrichment of the residency teaching program, and cost savings, by allowing more time to be spent in research, scholarly activities, and procedures.

Table 4-4 gives a breakdown of the internal medicine beds of the entire Detroit medical center.[24] The service is divided into A beds (resident teaching beds) and B beds (nonteaching physician assistant beds); the B beds comprise nearly half of the general internal medicine beds in the center and are covered by physician assistant housestaff.

At Harper Hospital, prior to the changeover to physician assistants, the 332 medical beds were covered by 20 interns, or PG-Is; 10 PG-IIs; and 10 PG-IIIs.* The average caseload for an intern was 16.6 patients. After changing to the new staffing pattern, 232 of these beds are covered by physician assistants, leaving the 100-bed teaching service staffed by eight interns and four PG-IIIs, an average of 12.5 patients per intern. PG-IIs have been shifted to medical subspecialty rotations. Physician assistant coverage of the 232-bed B service is provided by ten physician assistants working day hours and two physician assistants working evenings. Attending physicians and senior medical residents provide supervision and consultation. A moonlighting house physician provides evening and weekend backup coverage. Table 4-5 compares the costs for the medical service at Harper Hospital before and after the adoption of physician assistant-augmented internal medicine housestaff.[24] Costs for resident coverage before the addition of physician assistants were calculated on the basis of actual time spent by the resident in patient care ward coverage. Hence, the cost per year on the service is higher than

Table 4-4 Distribution of General Internal Medicine Beds in the Detroit Medical Center

	A[a]	B[b]	Total[c]
H-G-H Hospitals			
Harper Hospital	100	232	332
Hutzel Hospital	50	84	134
Grace Hospital	50	80	130
Detroit Receiving Hospital	100	0	100
VA Medical Center	100	0	100
Total	400	396	796

[a]A Beds = teaching beds (resident).
[b]B Beds = nonteaching beds (PA).
[c]Excludes specialty wards and intensive care units.

*PG = postgraduate (medical school) year of training.

Table 4-5 Costs of Coverage of General Medical Service, Harper Hospital   *

Position	Old Number Required	Cost per Service Year ($)[a]	Expenditure ($)
	Resident Coverage		
PG–I	20	29,600	592,000
PG–II	10	30,540	305,330
PG–III	10	47,200	472,200
Total			1,369,530

Position	Old Number Required	Transitional Cost per Service Year ($)[a]	Expenditure ($)
	Resident/PA Coverage		
PG–I	8	29,600	236,800
PG–II	4	30,533	122,132
PG–III	4	47,200	188,800
Subtotal, resident coverage			547,760
Physician assistants	12	33,706	404,472
House physician backup			112,320
Total			$1,064,524

Total Costs of Medical Service

Resident coverage	$1,396,530
Resident/physician assistant coverage	1,064,524
Cost savings to service	305,006

[a]Derived from actual cost of service to ward for 1 year, i.e., PG$ = I salary of $22,200 for 9 months coverage × .75 = $29,600 service/cost per year.

the salary of the resident, because PG-Is and PG-IIs spend only 9 months in ward coverage and a PG-III spends only 6 months. With the addition of the 12 physician assistants (with moonlighting physician backup) the need for resident coverage was reduced, resulting in an overall savings to the program and institution of over $300,000.

In terms of the nonmonetary advantages, the authors indicate the following additional benefits gained by the use of physician assistants in this model.

- adjustment of internal medicine teaching program to meet both educational and service demands
- restructuring of PG-II year into a series of mandatory subspecialty rotations
- increased continuity of care on the physician assistant service
- improved faculty/resident ratio

The authors conclude that the adoption of a physician assistant-augmented resident staff has produced significant benefits for this large internal medicine teaching program and has permitted not only flexibility in adjusting the residency program to meet educational demands and provide ongoing quality patient care but has also resulted in appreciable cost savings.[24] This remarkable success was anticipated by Dr. Eugene Stead in 1981.

> In many hospitals the physician assistant now performs functions formerly delegated to interns and residents. If working conditions are satisfactory and the physician assistant remains a part of the doctor's team, the doctor/physician assistant team may provide more units of service than the traditional doctor/intern team. The use of the physician assistant on the hospital service has allowed chiefs of services to be honest. For the first time they have the manpower and hands to cover service functions. They can reduce the resident/intern staffs without destroying needed service activity. They can more precisely define the number of interns and residents they need to have for educational purposes.[25]

The advantage that physician assistant utilization offers to residency programs in terms of balancing service demands with educational experiences is potentially very significant in the present-day climate of overproduction of specialists. Silver and McAtee have recently pointed out this advantage and have recommended that a national advisory committee representing various specialty training groups, physician assistant and nurse practitioner educators, and manpower planners be formed, to consider planning for the changing patterns of graduate medical education for both physicians and nonphysicians.[23]

Another example of physician assistant utilization in the housestaff role comes from the Norwalk Hospital, a 400-bed Yale-affiliated community hospital in southern Connecticut. This institution phased out its physician surgical residency in the late 1970s and replaced it with physician assistants. This experience has been carefully evaluated and reported.[26] At present there are 30 physician assistants on the surgical staff who function with attending physicians in the care of surgical patients. The Chief of Surgery at Norwalk, Dr. Malcolm S. Beinfield, states:

Residencies are a fiscal drag, and with the glut of surgeons, surgical residencies will be cut back. But hospitals' service needs will have to be met by someone. I see them being met by physician assistants. This wasn't planned as part of an overall cost-control movement, but it has worked out that way.[27]

The Norwalk experience has been replicated in a number of institutions throughout the country with equally positive results. The chief executive officer of the Euclid (Ohio) General Hospital, which has had 5 years of experience with the physician assistant housestaff concept, and in 1986 employed 25 physician assistants in medicine and surgery, states that "these are full-time employees and they're highly prized. Our physicians applaud their commitment to their work, and they fit in beautifully."[27]

The percentage of physician assistants working in hospitals has grown quickly since 1980 and as of 1986 physician assistants comprised over 30 percent of all practicing physician assistants. There seems to be a continuing strong demand for physician assistants in this setting, and their roles continue to expand into such specialty fields as emergency and trauma services, burns and plastic surgery, oncology, neonatology, cardiology, organ transplant services, neurology, orthopedics, ENT, urology, and geriatrics.

It would therefore seem that physician assistants offer considerable financial and nonfinancial benefits to community hospitals and academic medical centers and that these benefits are becoming increasingly apparent to physicians and administrators.

Noneconomic Benefits of Physician Assistant Utilization

It is clear that the employment of physician assistants by practices and hospitals results in their generating revenue that, at a minimum, is sufficient to cover the costs of their employment and, at a maximum, is sufficient to return a profit for employers. It has been shown on several occasions that practices employing physician assistants see more patients, generate more practice revenue, and create a higher physician net income than non-physician assistant practices.[12,19] There are also a number of noneconomic advantages to the utilization of physician assistants, advantages that are attractive and beneficial to both employers, patients, and society and do not readily show up in equations of cost effectiveness.

Education and Orientation

Because the major employers and supervisors of physician assistants are physicians, it is a relevant consideration that physician assistants are trained for the most part in the medical model. Most of the training is done by physicians and graduate physician assistants. Thus, they are oriented from the earliest stages of their education to develop skills and knowledge that are most helpful to physicians in medical diagnosis, treatment, and other tasks that will result in more efficient patient care. Related to this point is the apparent wide versatility of physician assistants. Even though they are trained in programs that largely emphasize primary care, they seem to move easily into roles in specialty and subspecialty areas with little or no additional formal training.[28] Thus, the skills of a physician assistant are readily applicable to clinical practice, and they are prepared to work closely with physicians in nearly all practice settings.

Practice in Underserved Areas

From the inception of the profession it was the intention that physician assistants would contribute to improving the delivery of medical care services to rural and underserved areas. It is widely acknowledged that physician assistants have fulfilled this intention and indeed have improved access to care in many regions across the country.[10,29] It has been shown that physician assistants are more likely than physicians to practice in rural and underserved communities.[29] Over one-third of clinically active physician assistants practice in communities of less than 50,000 population. Leiken examined patterns of physician assistant distribution in New York State and found that, compared to physicians, physician assistants tend to locate in counties that are underserved, small, aged, and poor.[30] Surveys of physician assistants in other areas of the country reveal similar results. Results from studies of recent graduates showed that 72 percent of physician assistants graduated in Kansas,[31] 80 percent of the graduates surveyed in Wisconsin,[32] and 43 percent of graduates surveyed in Iowa[33] were working in communities of fewer than 20,000 population. Therefore, physician assistants seem to gravitate toward practice areas in which there are more medical needs.

Quality of Care

Repeated studies consistently show that the quality of care delivered by physician assistants is equivalent to that of physicians.[14] In analyses of both process and outcome of care, physician assistants render care the quality of which cannot be distinguished from that of physician care in the primary care setting. The research findings on physician assistant quality of care have been so consistently positive that the Congressional Budget Office in 1979 recommended that no new studies in this area were required.[10]

Clinical Adaptability

One of the more remarkable features of the evolution of the physician assistant profession is that, although the initial focus of training was in primary care, a substantial number of these professionals have entered careers in specialty and subspecialty medicine. This professional movement was fostered by marketplace forces that affected the demand for health manpower.[18] These trends have shown that physician assistants are well prepared to practice not only in the field of primary care but also have little difficulty in adapting to roles in the inpatient setting, not infrequently in such specialty areas as cardiothoracic surgery, neonatology, plastic surgery, occupational medicine, and numerous others. This clinical adaptability makes them quite attractive to physician employers and hospital services. It also indicates a willingness on the part of physician assistants to work as part of a health care team, whether that be in a large group practice, HMO, or hospital staff. As dependent practitioners, physician assistants fit in well in the organizational structure of health delivery systems and function effectively as members of a team (i.e., residents, attendings, faculty) responsible for patient care.

Continuity of Care

In the discussion of physician assistant utilization in the hospital setting it was noted that employers perceived continuity of care as a major benefit of their employment. Unlike residents and fellows in the hospital setting, physician assistants remain on the services on which they work for long periods of time. Thus, they not only tend to become more familiar with the patients but also may be more effective employees in terms of awareness of established protocols and compliance with medical record requirements and physician preferences in diagnostic workups.

Empirical Basis of Physician Assistant Cost Effectiveness

It seems logical that, if physician assistants were not at least minimally cost effective, they would not be hired by practices and health care institutions. That they are in demand speaks to strong empirical evidence that these providers can "pay their way" in today's cost-conscious health care system.

Although it was felt in some quarters that the demand for physician assistants would decline as the nation entered a period of physician surplus,[34] there is little evidence that this is in fact taking place. Demand for physician assistants, in the mid-1980s, as evidenced by employment ads for physician assistants in national newspapers and journals, telephone inquiries to physician assistant training programs from persons seeking to hire physician assistants, and the low level of physician assistant unemployment reported in recent national surveys,[15] seems to be strong with no signs of any decline. This suggests that, even in a period of an oversupply of physicians, many practices and institutions perceive an ongoing role for physician assistants in health care delivery. The specific reasons why these employers continue to seek physician assistant services involve not only the economic benefits of their utilization but also some of the noneconomic benefits as well. In many instances, physician assistants work in settings that physicians have tended to avoid, i.e. occupational medicine, correctional medicine, geriatrics, rural areas, etc. In other circumstances, they have assumed surgical resident housestaff positions, allowing residency directors to limit the production of surgical specialists in some locales while maintaining a high level of surgical patient care. In the private practice setting, many physician assistants have assumed administrative and management functions that complement and expand their contribution to these practices. There are also a number of intangible benefits that accompany physician assistant utilization in these settings, such as commitment to the underserved, willingness to assume routine patient care duties, and willingness to function in a team role. These attributes are common among physician assistants and apparently influence their employers favorably. It would seem that these qualities often supersede purely economic factors in terms of perceptions of value of a physician assistant.

CONCLUSION

Cost effectiveness is but one attribute of the incorporation of physician assistants into medical practice. As emphasized, there are numerous other considerations and perceived benefits to the utilization of these health professionals. Vladeck makes the point that cost-effectiveness analysis is presently very trendy. As he states,

> Arguing cost effectiveness, rather than service quality or simple humanity, may sell more readily in the current political environment and may give the advocate a sense of personal sophistication and hardheadedness. But, a single-minded preoccupation with cost effectiveness to the exclusion of other criteria can be damaging and even self-defeating.[35]

Physician assistants provide not only clear economic advantages to practices and hospitals but also offer a number of other tangible and intangible benefits. In pondering the overall question of the value of the physician assistant concept and its worth to the medical community and the general public, all of these considerations must be weighed.

Past analyses of the cost effectiveness of physician assistants and of other mid-level health professions frame the question in terms of who benefits from this attribute. Is it the physician employer of the physician assistant, the patient, or society as a whole? The federal government has invested large sums to train physician assistants over the past 15 years, yet the utilization patterns of physician assistants are largely determined by physicians and the medical marketplace. Physician assistants do not by themselves determine their cost effectiveness. It is determined by the ways in which employing practices utilize them. The rationale of government subsidy of physician assistant training was to promote increased access of quality medical care to patients, and this objective continues to be met. It is met, however, through the utilization of physician assistants as employees of physicians and hospitals who are willing to assume the financial investment in hiring these professionals and who rightly benefit from these decisions. It may be naive in the entrepreneurial medical care system of the 1980s to expect that the direct cost-savings benefits of using physician assistants would accrue to anyone else. However, the use of physician assistants indirectly benefits patients by increasing access to care and providing a better quality of care at, in some cases, lower prices. Physician assistant employment in organized settings may result in lower medical care costs, as well as expansion of services.

This chapter has not directly addressed the costs of training physician assistants; however, it is clear that it is far less expensive than physician education. From a public policy perspective, it would seem that the government's investment in physician assistant training has been a sound and economic one, given their level of clinical capabilities and performance, their contribution to improvements in patient care, their relatively short preparation time, their willingness to work in underserved areas, and their adaptability to team approaches in health care. That physician assistant cost effectiveness (profitability) accrues to employers is a circumstance no different from other types of federally funded and initiated programs where the direct benefits of the project or product go to the private sector (in this instance, physicians and hospitals).

The overall value of physician assistant health manpower cannot be measured in strictly economic terms. The creation of the concept—an investment not only of the federal government but also of organized medicine and the educational sector—has provided numerous benefits to many groups—physicians, patients, health institutions, as well as society as a whole. Cost-effectiveness analyses often conclude by posing complex value judgments that fall in the domain of public policy decisions. In that context, given the past experience with physician assistants, it seems quite easy not only to justify their existence as high-level health care providers but also to argue for their continued integration into medical care practice.

NOTES

1. W.O. Spitzer, "The Nurse Practitioner Revisited: Slow Death of a Good Idea," *New England Journal of Medicine* 310(1984):1049–1051.

2. H.D. Banta and C.J. Beheny, "Technology Assessment," in *Public Health and Preventive Medicine*, 12th ed., ed. J.M. Last (Norwalk, CT: Appleton-Century-Crofts, 1986).

3. J.C. Record, M. McCally, S.O. Schweiter, et al., "New Health Professionals After a Decade and a Half: Delegation, Productivity and Costs in Primary Care," *Journal of Health Politics, Policy and Law* 5(1980):470–497.

4. R.E. Johnson, D.K. Freeborne, and M. McCally, "Delegation of Office Visits to PAs," *Physician Assistant* 9(1985):159–169.

5. J.E. Ott, *A Demonstration Project on the Education and Utilization of Child Health Associates and Their Impact on Medical Practice, Executive Summary.* 1979. Division of Medicine, CT. #231–75–0006.

6. R.M. Scheffler, "The Productivity of New Health Practitioners: Physician Assistants and MEDEX," *Research in Health Economics* 1(1979):37–48.

7. R.C. Mendenhall, et al., "Assessing the Utilization and Productivity of Nurse Practitioners and Physician Assistants: Methodology and Findings on Productivity," *Medical Care* 18(1980):609.

8. R.D. Carter, H.B. Perry, and D. Oliver, *Secondary Analysis: The 1981 National Survey of Physician Assistants* (Arlington, VA: Association of Physician Assistant Programs, 1984).

9. D.A. Crozier and J.K. Inglehart, "Trends in Health Manpower (Data Watch)," *Health Affairs* 3(1984):122–131.

10. *Physician Extenders: Their Current Role in Medical Care Delivery.* 1979. Congressional Budget Office, U.S. Congress.

11. Health Services Research Center, University of North Carolina at Chapel Hill, *The National Rural Primary Care Evaluation Project: Issue-Oriented Data Analysis/Final Report to the Robert Wood Johnson Foundation* (Chapel Hill, NC: Health Services Research Center, April 1985).

12. *Survey and Evaluation of the Physician Extender Reimbursement Experiment, Final Report.* Contract #SSA-600-76-D167 (System Sciences, Inc., 1978). US Dept of Health and Human Services.

13. L. LeRoy, *Case Study #16: The Costs and Effectiveness of Nurse Practitioners, in The Implications of Cost-Effectiveness Analysis of Medical Technology, Background Paper #2: Case Studies of Medical Technology.* 1981. Office of Technology Assessment, U.S. Congress.

14. H.C. Sox, "Quality of Patient Care by Nurse Practitioners and Physician Assistants: A Ten Year Perspective," *Annals of Internal Medicine* 91(1979):459–472.

15. G. Schafft, "Masterfile Survey 1984—PAs in Specialties," *AAPA News* 6(1985):4.

16. Miller and Byrne, Inc., *Review and Analysis of State Legislation and Reimbursement Practice, Final Report.* 1978. US Dept of Health and Human Services.

17. J.L. Weston, "Ambiguities Limit the Role of Nurse Practitioners and Physician Assistants," *American Journal of Public Health* 74(1984):6–7.

18. J.F. Cawley, J.E. Ott, and C. DeAtley, "The Future for Physician Assistants," *Annals of Internal Medicine* 98(1983):993–997.

19. American Medical Association, Center for Health Policy Research, *SMS Report*, Vol. 1, No. 10, December 1982, p. 10.

20. G. Greenfield, A.L. Komaroff, T.M. Pass, et al., "Efficiency and Cost of Primary Care by Nurses and Physicians," *New England Journal of Medicine* 298(1978):305–309.

21. E. Poirier-Elliot, "Cost-Effectiveness of Non-physician Health Care Professionals," *Nurse Practitioner* 7(1984):54–56.

22. G.M. Scharon and E.J. Bernacki. "A Corporate Role for Nurse Practitioners," *Business and Health*, September 1984, pp. 26–27.

23. H.K. Silver and D.A. McAtee. "On the Use of Nonphysician 'Associate Residents' in Over-crowded Specialty Training Programs," *New England Journal of Medicine* 311(1984):326–328.

24. J.E. Frick. "The Urban Health Care Setting: The Harper-Grace Hospital Experience," in S.F. Zarbock and K. Harbert (eds.), *Physician Assistants: Present and Future Models of Utilization* (New York: Praeger Publishing Co., 1986), p. 91.

25. E. Stead, "The Physician Assistant and Internal Medicine," *American Journal of Medicine* 70(1981):1161–1162.

26. J.J. Heinrich, et al., "The Physician Assistant as Resident on Surgical Services," *Archives of Surgery* 115(1980):310–314.

27. M. Mamber, "NPs, MDs, and PAs: Meshing Their Changing Roles," *Medical World News*, September 23, 1985.

28. J.F. Cawley, "The Physician Assistant Profession: Current Status and Future Trends," *Journal of Public Health Policy* 6(1985):78–99.

29. H.B. Perry and B. Breitner, *Physician Assistants: Their Contribution to Health Care* (New York: Human Sciences Press, 1981).

30. A.M. Leiken, "Factors Affecting the Distribution of Physician Assistants in New York State: Policy Implications," *Journal of Public Health Policy* 6(1985):236–243.

31. S.C. Gladhart, et al., "The Physician Assistant in Kansas," *Journal of the Kansas Medical Society* 79(1978):20.

32. F. Lohrenz, et al., "Placement of Primary Care Physician Assistants in Small Rural Communities," *Wisconsin Medical Journal* 75(1976):593–595.

33. D. Oliver, et al., "Distribution of Primary Care Physician Assistants in the State of Iowa," *Journal of the Iowa Medical Society* 67(1977):320.

34. *Report of the Graduate Medical Education National Advisory Committee (GMENAC)*. 1980. US Dept of Health and Human Services.

35. B.C. Vladeck, "The Limits of Cost-Effectiveness," *American Journal of Public Health* 74(1984):652–653.

Chapter 5

The Physician Assistant and Public Health Issues

Molly Backup is a physician assistant who practices in a rural HMO. She has been active for a number of years in the American Public Health Association and gives the authors her opinions about the role physician assistants can play in public health.

Gretchen Schafft: What do you think is a good definition of public health?

Molly Backup: The public's health encompasses more than individual diseases and individual cures. It means an epidemiologic approach to disease. It means the community, whether at a state or county or federal level, combating disease and promoting health measures by improving sanitation or controlling infectious disease. Generally, however, all of these activities have the theme that public health involves more than a specific illness and a specific disease that is treated through a standard diagnosis and cure methodology.

Gretchen Schafft: Public health has been defined simply as social justice. What do you think of that point of view?

Molly Backup: Health status has so much to do with one's position, one's income, living situation, job, satisfaction with life that it's clear that all the efforts we make with curative medicine have less to do with the overall health status than the living standard of the individual. If you look at correlations between health and variables affecting health, what correlates the highest is living standard.

Gretchen Schafft: Where do you think the physician assistant fits into the domain of public health?

Molly Backup: One role that I think we as physician assistants are suited for is prevention through health education about the specific diseases and problems that patients bring to the medical practice as they're coming in for more routine kinds of examinations and counseling. For instance, the patient who comes in with bronchitis presents a perfect opportunity to talk not only about the treatment of bronchitis but also about the elimination of those risk factors for future bronchitis, such as exposure to dust or other irritants at work or at home or smoking. It is possible to include as indicated such things as appropriate immunizations for flu or getting the pneumonia vaccine. Some physician assistants are good at leading groups on such topics as nonsmoking or stress management. I think it's also important for health professionals in general to be involved in helping set standards of what is appropriate in health care and also in such areas as exposure at work to hazards.

Gretchen Schafft: Helping the public become aware of the total impact of the environment on health and illness, is that it?

Molly Backup: I think that some of the health promotion is geared toward the specific patient. But I think that if that's all that we do, if we don't get involved in helping change how health care can be distributed, how society's resources can be distributed better to ensure the public's health, that we are not doing as much as we can in the area of public health. In public health circles the definition of what is a threat to the public's health is fairly broad and includes even the threat of extinction posed by nuclear disasters and war, the trauma caused by fears that kids growing up now have about nuclear war, and the expenditures of our resources in development of nuclear weapons instead of health and social services. All of those are included as areas of concern about public health. It's not the standard definition of health care. It's a much broader perspective, and most people in public health have this broader perspective.

Gretchen Schafft: Do you think that physician assistants could become better prepared as public health advocates?

Molly Backup: I think that one role that physician assistants can fill is to continue our work as health promoters and to enhance it with a greater awareness of public health issues and by becoming involved in policy development. Public health issues are not as high on the physician assistant's priorities as I would like them to be. I do think that physician assistants do spend more time talking to patients, educating them about their specific disease, and telling them about their medicines. However, on some of the broader issues, I'd say physician assistants probably are wary of many public health issues. There are many physician assistants who work specifically in jobs that are within public health, such as drug abuse clinics, sexually transmitted disease clinics, occupational health clinics, and correctional medicine. Some work in institutional settings that are run by the Public Health Service. I think one of the things that has been difficult for some physician assistants working in that field is that many jobs funded through public health dollars have been cut from the federal, state, and local budgets.

I think it behooves us to start thinking in those broader senses of health policy about where health care really is going. I think there will be a national health program, and I would hope, as part of that national health program, that disease prevention will be the primary focus. I also hope we'll see occupational health care as an important part of it. This would really advance efforts to both provide high-quality health care and to save costs. And physician assistants are ideal to provide a lot of these health care services that require medical knowledge and also interaction skills. We aren't as costly as physicians in providing those services, and we often have better training in health promotion and patient counseling. But if we don't take an active part in working and planning where health care is going to go in this country, we may not be part of the new direction.

THE PHYSICIAN ASSISTANT AND PUBLIC HEALTH ISSUES

Public health is the centripetal force in medicine. It is at the center of the health care system and pulls all health care interests and activities, no matter how remote, back toward it because it not only reflects but also actually determines the health status of the nation. If public health is a low priority of a nation, eventually all other areas of public life suffer. As experience in the Third World has shown, even those who can afford unlimited health care are affected by lack of sanitation, rampant disease, and epidemics and endemic illnesses that fester among the masses.

What do we mean by public health? Public health is a more inclusive field than medicine. It concerns itself with the health of population groups, not individuals. It is often multidisciplinary in its interests and approaches. Historically, it stems from two very diverse fields: social work and industrial hygiene and currently is closely tied to epidemiology and microbiology. Public health is often viewed as a philosophy, as a movement of social reform or, in the broadest sense, as social justice itself, for the health of the public is based on the social and physical environment in which we live.[1]

This chapter examines the relevance of public health to the careers of physician assistants and explores some of the public health problems that are most pressing in today's society. An aspect of public health concern—providing health care to the underserved—was discussed in Chapter 3.

HISTORY OF THE PUBLIC HEALTH FIELD

The American public health movement grew out of the English reform movements of the mid-1800s. Disease and pestilence seemed to be an integral part of the Industrial Revolution, which brought large numbers of people in close contact with one another under conditions that fostered illness and disease. A few public leaders recognized the connection between poverty, dirt, and epidemics and called for a campaign to clean up all of England, and the streets of London in particular.

Most innovations in England moved rapidly to the United States in the Colonial period, and this trend continued after independence. By 1870, Massachusetts had adopted the English innovation of government oversight of health conditions and inaugurated a State Board of Health that was charged with keeping health records, developing sanitation programs, working toward a better environment for the highly populated areas, and developing services for women and children that would improve their health status. This idea spread throughout the states, and one after another developed local health authorities and state health departments.

When the U.S. Public Health Service came into being in 1912 it built upon the system of public health hospitals, established as the Marine Hospital Service in

1798 to provide health care for seamen who had no permanent residence. The U.S. Public Health Service remains today a source of research initiatives to improve the health of the population, a font of services that reach into all areas of the country, and a recipient of health care data that can be analyzed and disseminated throughout the country to inform citizens of the state of the public's health.

For over a century private citizens have been interested in public health as well and in sharing information about it. The first meeting of the American Public Health Association was held in 1873, and by 1911 it had a journal and five standing sections, four of which remain as part of the association today. These five sections were the laboratory, health officers, statistics, sanitary engineering, and sociological sections. Only the sociological section has been dropped from the current association.[2]

In a literature content review of the *American Journal of Public Health,* the editor notes that articles near the turn of the century dealt more frequently with sanitation and articles about medicine came to predominate in the last 30 years.[3] Similar topics were presented in the other medical journals of the age. Only after a sanitation system became the norm in American life did that interest decline.

The idea, however, that public health problems are rooted in social and environmental conditions continues to this day. Many of the articles in current journals of public health express concerns for pollutants, social behaviors that increase health problems, effects of socioeconomic conditions on occurrence of illness, and the potential for nuclear war as a result of sociopolitical beliefs and actions.

Medical care is based on the premise that one individual (a health care provider) can help another individual (a patient) to achieve health and overcome illness. Public health is based on the idea that agencies can create conditions in which the health of populations can be enhanced and disease avoided or controlled. Public health involves collective action and, to some degree, coercion. To be effective, it requires a redistributive force through which the public good will dictate limits on entrepreneurial activities and self-interest in the larger interest of the public. (The tension between issues of equity and issues of marketplace economics in this discussion was described in detail in Chapter 1.) One author describes the public health egalitarian vision as follows:[4]

- controlling the hazards of the world
- preventing death and disability through organized collective action shared equally by all except where unequal burdens exist
- resulting in increased protection of everyone's health, especially potential victims of death and disability

The rest of this chapter examines three areas of concern to public health: the growth of technology and the access of the public to the benefits it promises, new illnesses and diseases that threaten the health of the nation, and the growth of the health promotion/disease prevention movement in which physician assistants will play an important role.

TECHNOLOGICAL ADVANCES AND PUBLIC HEALTH

Public health is based on the idea that primary care is the foundation of sound medical care for the population at large and, therefore, for the overall health of the nation. As a result, unbridled technology is not always viewed with great sympathy by public health practitioners and advocates. Rapid growth of technology can be costly, unproven in its effectiveness, and not always useful in preventive medicine.[5] It can divert resources from programs that have wide application and significant impact on the nation's health and from the provision of primary care.

The kinds of technology that are most appreciated by the adherents of the public health movement are those that can enhance the food supply, reduce the effect of toxic waste, facilitate population control, or prevent disease through vaccination. Of less interest are those technological innovations that will affect only a few people in the population, create system-wide expenses, and improve longevity but not the quality of life.

There is no consensus about how rapidly technology is moving through our medical care system. Representatives of the pharmaceutical industry, because of the lengthy time required for approval of new drugs from the Food and Drug Administration and the very high cost of their development, feel that innovation is costly and risky. On the other hand, the 25,000 medical device-related patents that have been granted since 1960 represent advances in both "little ticket technologies" and "big ticket technologies"; they range from new kinds of laboratory tests to new techniques in treating myocardial infarction.[6,7]

Public health personnel are very concerned about the appropriateness of the technology that is introduced. A technology can be considered appropriate if its value to society is equal to or less than its cost. One well-known health economist believes that such technology may be hard to find. According to his logic, the technological advances, in order to be cost effective, must *replace* procedures that were previously more costly and must not generate direct or indirect costs that exceed the savings.[8] Because technologies save lives, the costs may be shifted to a future date, but illness and death cannot be avoided and indeed the life saved may be more costly to society than an earlier demise. This logic seems to indicate that it makes most sense to use technological advantages for those who are still economically productive, rather than the old or frail. However, what makes economic sense may not pass the test of public opinion.

Among the most costly of the new technologies are the organ transplants that have become common in the 1980s. The cost of liver, kidney, and heart transplants can run into the six figures, and these are seldom paid from out-of-pocket dollars. Insurance companies and federal programs are burdened disproportionately with the costs of these operations for the relatively small number of insurees who need them and obtain them. For instance, the federal government pays 100 percent of the costs of procurement of usable organs for these operations. Almost 7,000 kidneys were transplanted in 1984, with a waiting list of 1,400 during that year alone.[9] It is estimated that about half of the 74,000 kidney dialysis patients in the United States are candidates for a kidney transplant.[10]

The costs of organ transplant programs are enormous and must compete for health care dollars with other programs. If health care costs are not going to rise precipitously, then the increased costs of some programs must be balanced by decreased costs in others. There are certainly more candidates for increases than decreases.

Some technologies have enormous repercussions not only for sustaining life but also for enhancing the ability of people to live their lives in a more satisfactory manner. Some orthopedic surgery, for instance, can lead to a greater degree of comfort for arthritic patients or victims of broken hips. However, the fact that one can remain mobile and self-sufficient is important to society, as well as the individual, but does not negate the fact that there will be a period later on when disability, illness, and death will be likely and the ultimate probability.

Nor is there a sufficient amount of resources to serve all those who might like to take advantage of the latest and most expensive technology in health care. As has been mentioned, organ procurement is lagging behind the demand for organ transplants. The machinery available for diagnostic tests is not found in every locality or hospital. The out-of-pocket costs or co-payments associated with procedures using the new technologies may make it difficult for many patients to take advantage of them.

Eventually, the allocation of scarce resources must become part of the public debate over health care. The term "rationing" is offensive to some as it brings with it the image of the hard choices of wartime.[11] Whether one uses that term or the more innocuous term "allocation of resources," the reality is the same. Decisions will be made, either explicitly or implicitly, to provide access to the new technologies to some patients and not to others. How that will be done is the question.

Criteria that might be used in allocation of resources within the health care system might include ability to pay, or ability to adapt to the new requirements for home health care, or even being in the right place at the right time. In England such factors as age, other health complications, physical or mental disability, and lack of adequate facilities at home influence who receives kidney transplants. Similarly, treatment for cancer is more likely to be of the aggressive nature known in the United States if the patient is a child or a young person. Productivity of the individual is a consideration, at least in some instances, in determining the appropriate use of therapies in England.[12]

In the United States, the limitation on the use of medical technological advances is more likely to come as a result of cost to the individual than it is from the advice of the physician. Americans are not likely to take the advice of any health care provider to limit therapy if there is a known treatment that is not too risky or uncomfortable. There is so much information available through the media about technological advances that patients are likely to know a great deal about what is available. Yet, to pay personally for the treatment may be daunting. Or, if the treatment offers prolonged life, but at significant cost in terms of pain and discomfort, the decision may be made to forego the treatment. This response is embodied in the hospice movement in this country and abroad in which cancer patients decline further treatment in favor of a relatively pain-free final period of life.

The health of the public cannot be greatly enhanced by technologies that rob the coffers of the health care system for the benefit of a few. Maternal and child nutrition, pregnancy prevention, and protection from disease by vaccination are much more important to the larger numbers in our society than high-tech solutions to problems affecting only a few. However, as long as some can pay, there will be the urge to increase costly technology in health care, regardless of the consequences to the health of the nation as a whole.

For physician assistants, the new technologies offer a range of employment opportunities that fall within their expertise. Management of patient care involving the use of a particular device or piece of equipment is a growing reality. Educating the patient about care for such a procedure as dialysis may require a great deal of patient involvement. The use of technology can also bring more care into the home where the physician assistant can instruct the patient on the use of home equipment and help the patient develop ways of communicating with the office practice. However, the extensive use of physician assistants depends upon coverage of their services by government and private insurance. Such reimbursement remains inadequate, indeed virtually nonexistent, in the realm of home health care.

Technology often provides the answer to troublesome disease entities that plague a population. Tuberculosis, the scourge of the last century, is now a threat to only a small portion of the population. Polio, the killer and disabler of the middle of this century, is now a memory to public health workers. However, as one disease is controlled through new forms of treatment or prevention, another one, such as AIDS, may take its place.

NEW DISEASES AND MENACES

AIDS Epidemic

New diseases and public health menaces are numerous. In the mid-1980s, the worst threat to the world's health from infectious disease is posed by AIDS. It presents such a total drain on all segments of the health care system, from financing to health care services, that it is difficult to capture its enormity in a short discussion.

The first indication of this disease came to the attention of the medical community in 1981. Apparently healthy individuals presented with unusual malignancies, immune system deficiencies, and a wide variety of uncommon infections. As cases were reported to the Centers for Disease Control (CDC) in Atlanta, it became evident that young homosexual men were the primary victims of the disease. In 1982, the first evidence of the new disease was seen in hemophiliacs who received blood products pooled from thousands of donors. Following this discovery, intravenous drug users and female sexual partners of AIDS victims were added to the growing list of high-risk groups.[13]

The number of cases grew so fast that, by 1987, more than 33,000 cases had been reported to the Centers for Disease Control. Of these, 56 percent were already dead. Epidemiologists estimated 1987 incidence rates as low as .1 per 100,000 for people in nonrisk groups, but much higher for people in certain risk categories:[14,15]

Population-Specific Annual Incidence Rates, AIDS

Population	*Rate*
• Single men in Manhattan and San Francisco, IV drug users in New York City and New Jersey, persons with Hemophilia A	260–350/100,000
• U.S. citizens not in high-risk groups	>1/100,000
• Overall U.S. population	6/100,000
• Central Africa	17/100,000
• Switzerland and Denmark	1/100,000

Its spread has been so rapid that by 1991, according to the Institute of Medicine, it may be one of the ten leading causes of death.

AIDS, the acquired immune deficiency syndrome, encompasses a number of clinical representations of infection with a recently identified retrovirus, HIV (human immunodeficiency virus). This virus attacks human T lymphocytes and brain cells and is the causative agent of AIDS and related syndromes.

AIDS attacks not only the key immunologic cells of the body, but also damages cells of the central nervous system. In doing so, it causes a wide range of neurologic problems, the most severe of which is profound dementia.[16,17] It profoundly affects the immune system, weakening it to such an extent that susceptibility to unusual kinds of infection, such as mycobacterium avium and coccidioidomycosis, follows.

The progression of the disease has become familiar to most physician assistants. Diagnosis is often made when a life-threatening opportunistic infection, such as pneumocystis carinii pneumonia (PCP), Kaposi's sarcoma (KS), Burkitt's lymphoma, or a primary lymphoma of the central nervous system, is found. When a person is exposed to AIDS, he or she may remain asymptomatic for a period of time, even years; but at this asymptomatic stage, infected persons may be more contagious than when they develop the symptoms. The contagious stage can occur even when the infection has not been present long enough to show up in antibody tests.

The impact of AIDS on health care personnel is felt in many ways. Medical training and experience, particularly in high-incidence areas, is dominated by the disease. Cases seen in hospitals demand time and attention that would usually be devoted to a broader spectrum of concerns during the clinical phase of a physician assistant's education. Particular attention must be paid to ensuring a safe work environment to reduce the chances of contamination.

To date, very few health care workers outside of the high-risk groups have contracted the HIV virus. Yet, their potential parenteral exposure and contact with the patient's body fluids are cause for extreme caution. Fortunately, there is little evidence that the virus is very transmissible other than through intimate human contact. Precautions taken by physician assistants to avoid exposure to hepatitis B are usually sufficient in reference to the AIDS infection as well. Cuts and skin lesions that might come into contact with the body fluids of AIDS patients should be protected by a covering. Gloves should be worn when handling any of the AIDS patients' blood, excretions, or other fluids. All blood should be labeled with special warnings, and containers should be disinfected with a 1:10 solution of bleach and water. Needle stick injuries should be avoided, and needles used for AIDS patients should be disposed of in puncture-resistant containers.[18]

The outlook for a cure for AIDS is not optimistic, nor is the prevention of the disease easy to achieve. Most feel it will be years before a vaccine to protect against AIDS will be available. Changes in sexual behavior patterns are occurring in the homosexual community as a consequence of AIDS, but the history of attempts to control other venereal diseases leads one to believe that a vaccine will be a more effective solution than behavioral change.

The nature of AIDS is such that finding a quick cure for it is particularly unlikely. Medicine has not had much success in coping with viral infections in general. The HIV virus is particularly complex as, according to a recent review, it "integrates itself into the DNA of the host cell and affects cellular material in the immunologic system. For those who are already sick it would be necessary to restore the compromised immune system. These tasks involve frontier work in immunology and virology."[19]

Nor has treatment offered much relief to infected persons with severe symptoms. Azothiapoin (AZT) appears to have some effect on the progress of the disease. Interferon and Interleukin-2 have been tried, but with little success. Children with AIDS are being given immunoglobulins. Because of its widespread effect on the immune and nervous systems, there is no single solution to the treatment of the viral disease short of a vaccine that would halt its development.[20] Investigation of possible vaccines are underway in centers throughout the country and abroad.

AIDS patients have a wide variety of symptoms, problems, and needs. They are psychologically affected by the stigma attached to the lifestyle that may be identified with the acquisition of the disease. They may also be shunned because of the fear that has been engendered in the population of this seemingly incurable illness. At the time of diagnosis, many AIDS patients have to tell their loved ones of their homosexuality, as well as of their impending fate. This burdens not only the patient but the family members as well. The depressed and confused mental state of the patient may be due to this stress or to the illness itself, which causes severe neurologic changes in many of its victims.

AIDS patients show a continuum of physical and mental symptoms that may be insignificant to debilitating. For those who are functioning well, there is no reason to give up work and other activities, although extreme caution should be taken to avoid spreading the disease through sexual practices that put others at risk. Unfortunately, there is such fear of the AIDS patient that many employers find cause to dismiss the employee with this illness. Loss of a job adds to the distress and inability of the patient to cope with the costs of care and the independence needed for continued self-esteem.

The physician assistant's training and skills enable him or her to play a role in ameliorating the public health threat posed by AIDS. Perhaps the first duty of the physician assistant is to become as informed as possible about this illness both for the sake of preventing contamination of the health care environment and for finding rational ways to inform the public about the nature of AIDS. For those physician assistants in clinical practice, the presentation of the symptoms of AIDS will be important to recognize, and ways of informing patients that they have the disease should be examined in order to provide the most supportive care possible. Each physician assistant in practice should know what facilities are available in the community to provide ongoing social, psychological, and financial support to the AIDS patient. Each should know the advice that should be provided to all patients regarding how to avoid the further spread of the disease.

Physician assistants may see some AIDS patients as part of their regular clinical responsibilities, and a few may even find their careers devoted to helping solve this public health problem for a period of time. Organizing health care services in areas of population density of high-risk individuals will involve some physician assistants. Others may become involved in the psychological support systems of the clinics dealing with AIDS. Others may work in hospital wards or units devoted to AIDS patients. Finally, the role of home health care is certain to grow as the financial burden of the disease leads health care planners to urge outpatient care in all appropriate cases to cut costs. Sharing information with members of the profession and other health professionals about the care that they are providing to these patients will be increasingly important as the physician assistant continues the role of health provider to those most in need.

Nuclear War as a Public Health Issue

Unlike the epidemic of AIDS, which at this time is limited to defined risk groups with only small numbers of the population outside these groups involved, another problem is being defined as a public health menace that affects the entire population, although it kills no one at the present time. Nuclear war presents the possibility of elimination of the human race as we know it and is considered by some of the leaders in the public health movement to be the most pressing of all problems. It has been addressed in the American Public Health Association President's annual inaugural address, summary of the year, or policy statements in each year from 1981–1986. At the 1986 Annual Meeting of the American Public Health Association, 525 persons attending the conference in Las Vegas, Nevada, demonstrated at the Nevada Nuclear Test Site on the day of an underground nuclear test. Of the demonstrators, 139 were arrested for entering the area where the test would actually take place only a few hours before the detonation.

What is the origin of such concern expressed by health professionals? In 1986 two technological disasters shook the faith of many in the invincible nature of "progress." The Challenger space shuttle self-destructed in flight, and the accident at the Chernobyl nuclear power plant contaminated an unknown area of land, people, and other life forms extending across national boundaries. The imperative need to monitor and reverse policies that place the health of the public at unacceptable risk roused many public health people to action.

One of the functions of public health advocates is to inform the public of environmental hazards. Often the public is not receptive to the news. In terms of the nuclear threat, the information that needs to be shared is both the actual outcome of nuclear war, as assessed by scientific research and medical experience, and the costs of supporting the nuclear war industry, which divert funds from other governmental programs, including health care.

The amount of money that is diverted from other national needs by military expenditures is enormous. It is estimated that one-tenth of the annual military budgets of the United States and the Soviet Union would provide immunizations, safe water supplies, and basic adequate food for the children of the Third World, who are estimated to die at the rate of 40,000 every 24 hours, or 15 million a year.[21] Converting the military-industrial complex into the peaceful-industrial complex is not an easy task, but many public health people are in the forefront of urging just such a reassessment of priorities.

The concepts of the "limited nuclear war" and the "survivable nuclear war" have been refuted by public health leaders among others. The death of people in the path of nuclear strikes would surely be followed by destruction of the food supplies for the survivors, the contamination of future food and water supplies, deterioration in the quality of the soil, and the climatic effects of the nuclear war.[22] There is now an enormous body of literature supporting all of these assertions.

Although there are no refutations of the potential for disaster from nuclear war, there remains a large silent majority of people who choose not to address these issues and who trust to luck, faith in the world's leaders, and continuing technological defense mechanisms to keep the reality of war from their doorsteps. The position of the public health community is that we are obliged to be informed and act on conscience to inform the public about the nuclear threat in continuous and compelling ways.

Physician assistants have formed a link to Physicians for Social Responsibility, which is devoted to the prevention of nuclear war, through the Physician Assistants for Social Responsibility, a group that serves as a source of public information for the profession about the nuclear threat. It holds regular meetings and publishes a newsletter that is disseminated in every state where physician assistants practice. Its aim is to develop a network of concerned practitioners who can monitor policies and events related to nuclear proliferation and environmental hazards associated with the armaments race and present scenarios of results of nuclear conflict. Physician assistants, with their knowledge of the actual provision of health care, can contribute to a realistic portrayal of the results of nuclear confrontation as well. All national discussion of this vital topic can help to focus the public's attention on the real dangers of our age.

Substance Abuse and Public Health

Links between the nuclear threat and the substance abuse epidemic in the United States may be tenuous, but both point to an anomie that affects several areas of American life. The extent of drug use in the American culture is always open to debate because incidence figures depend on self-reporting, a notoriously poor measure. In the National Survey on Drug Abuse, conducted in 1982 by the Public Health Service, the incidence of marijuana use, the most heavily used illicit drug, was estimated at 64 percent "ever used" for the 18 to 25 age group.[23] There is evidence that the use of marijuana is related to life stages and that heavy usage often declines as the users marry and have children at home.

The National Survey also proposes a staging of a drug user's "career" with illicit substances. This career begins with alcohol and cigarette use, proceeds to marijuana, and then to use of "stage 3" drugs, such as cocaine, hallucinogens, and heroin, and abuse of psychotherapeutic drugs. More recently manufactured chemical compounds, such as "PCP," "Ecstasy," and "Crack," have been

102   THE PHYSICIAN ASSISTANT

introduced. Cheaply produced and widely distributed, these new drugs have
created their own epidemics.

It seems that people who use the "stage 3" drugs continue their use of other
substances as well. Almost all users of "hard drugs" report some continued use of
alcohol, cigarettes, or marijuana in some combination. Factors that are associated
with drug use are exposure to drug use in the family setting, early teenage dating,
and little involvement in family life. Race and sex are not good predictors of who
will become a drug user, but heavy use is found more frequently in boys than in
girls of the youthful groups.

The physician assistant profession is a young one, and has many practitioners
who themselves have been exposed to drug use and understand its allure and its
hazards. A recent issue of the *New England Journal of Medicine* reported that,
among medical students and physicians, 59 percent of the physicians and 78 percent of the students reported that they had used psychoactive drugs. Five percent of
the medical students reported drug dependence.[24] Although no such study has
been conducted for physician assistants, the results could be similar.

The numbers of practicing physician assistants who identify themselves as
belonging to Alcoholics Anonymous or Narcotics Anonymous is unknown. However, both groups hold meetings during the AAPA annual convention to support
their members in stressful and tempting away-from-home situations. A national
Task Force on the Impaired Practitioner, a project of AAPA, has developed
programs to bring physician assistants with substance abuse problems to treatment
and to help other practitioners understand the nature of drug dependency so that
they will be better able to help themselves and their patients. Accepting that there
is substance abuse within the profession is only to say that physician assistants are
part of the American culture. Providing attention to the issues of patient care in this
domain and responsible clinical caregiving are necessary steps in the maturation of
the profession.

Physician assistants are playing many important roles in drug abuse clinics and
similar facilities. In many hospitals, there are special clinical units for drug- and
substance-addicted patients. For the inpatient in a psychiatric ward, particularly
one with drug dependency problems, the physician assistant is a resource for
primary care and can assist in group therapy under the supervision of a psychia-
trist. In some hospitals, such as VA hospitals, the mental health team prefers that
the physical care of the patients be handled by a practitioner who is stationed on the
unit but is not directly involved in psychotherapeutic activities with the patients.

The recognition of severe drug reactions and overdoses is a primary task of the
physician assistant in emergency room care. In all of the settings mentioned, the
physician assistant is able to provide health education while conducting clinical
tasks.

HEALTH PROMOTION AND DISEASE PREVENTION

One of the goals of public health is the prevention of illness and disease through collective action on the part of governmental agencies and individual action by people to reduce health risks. In the past several years, the reduction in the incidence of heart disease and stroke can be directly related to actions taken by individuals to change their behavior to embrace healthier lifestyles. A constituency for health promotion/disease prevention activities is found among many individuals, in industry, and in the government as people and groups define their self-interest to be at stake in health promotion.

Physician assistants have always been trained to provide patient counseling in the realm of medical concerns. In certain physician assistant programs, a counseling and psychosocial orientation has been a strong focus of the educational curriculum.[25] Perhaps because there is less social distance between them and their patients than between patients and physicians, they have frequently assumed health education roles within their practices. It is also true that counseling of patients is not a reimbursable expense with most third party payers; thus, using the physician assistant to provide that service costs the practice less than if the physician took the same amount of time to provide patient education. When health education and prevention are incorporated into the regular medical care received by patients, the patient receives an integrated approach to wellness.

In the past, nurses were identified as the providers of patient education more frequently than physician assistants. Because data had not been systematically gathered about health promotion activities of physician assistants it was difficult to refute claims that nurses and nurse practitioners were more adept at health promotion activities than physician assistants. The 1985 Role Delineation Study of the AAPA was the first study based on detailed information to show the actual extent of physician assistant activities in health promotion and disease prevention.

There were 93 task items related to health promotion/disease prevention in the survey instrument. Through analysis of clusters of like responses, 13 areas of counseling emerged and were labeled by a group of physician assistant "experts." These clusters are:

1. pediatric preventive counseling
2. cardiovascular preventive counseling
3. patient education: aging and chronic mental illness
4. gynecologic and family planning counseling
5. pre- and postoperative patient education
6. patient education: medications and laboratory tests
7. prevention counseling and screening: eye and tooth
8. pediatric well-child counseling

   9. lifestyle counseling
10. general patient education
11. pediatric conditions counseling
12. community maintenance resources for the elderly
13. obstetrical patient education

Responses to questions about whether a particular problem was seen in the clinical practice by the respondent physician assistants indicated that physician assistants see an enormous variety of conditions involving every organ system. The respondents were also asked the level of their involvement in treating the conditions seen in the practice. Responses were scaled according to whether the physician assistant had (1) no responsibility, (2) gave information when requested by the patient, (3) recommended and encouraged the patient in a specific course of action, or (4) planned, supported, and counseled individual patients concerning a course of action.

Although some physician assistants may not have any occasion to counsel patients on problems not seen in their particular practice, the vast majority are taking responsibility for informing patients about healthy ways of life. More than 80 percent of the physician assistant respondents reported providing care in such areas as responding to stress, counseling smoking cessation, sexually transmitted disease prevention, drug and alcohol abuse education, and management of anxiety disorders.

Regarding the following specific health promotion/disease prevention activities, more than 50 percent of the physician assistant respondents indicated that they recommend a course of action and provide direct counseling support.

- diet and weight reduction
- exercise
- hypertension education
- immunizations
- obesity
- home safety and prevention of accidents
- prevention of poisoning
- proper nutrition
- responding to stress
- tobacco use
- use of seat belts and restraints

The effect of specialization upon the kind of health promotion/disease prevention activities engaged in by the physician assistant is significant, as can be seen in Table 5-1.

Table 5-1 Health Promotion Activity Clusters by Physician Assistant Specialty

Physician Assistant Specialty	Pediatric preventive counseling	Cardiovascular preventive counseling	Patient education: Aging and chronic/ mental illness	Gynecologic and family planning counseling	Pre- and postoperative patient education	Patient education: medications and lab tests	Preventive counseling: screen: eye and tooth	Pediatric (well-child) counseling	Lifestyle counseling	General patient education	Pediatric conditions counseling	Community maintenance resources for the elderly	Obstetrical patient education
Psychiatry	1.11	1.40	2.12	1.01	0.90	1.91	1.05	0.65	1.85	1.85	0.87	1.35	0.43
Family Gen	1.88	1.72	1.94	1.90	1.34	2.33	1.30	1.48	2.23	2.36	1.02	1.46	1.04
Pediatric	1.95	0.74	1.28	1.19	0.89	2.13	1.32	1.92	1.84	1.96	1.19	1.30	0.83
Geriatric	1.40	2.00	2.05	1.22	1.36	2.10	1.30	0.64	1.76	2.06	0.78	1.52	0.48
Intl Genl	1.45	1.88	1.74	1.35	0.83	2.18	1.04	0.60	2.00	2.08	0.70	1.17	0.44
Intl Spec	1.38	1.35	1.49	1.28	1.38	1.98	1.04	0.89	1.75	1.78	0.79	1.15	0.72
Emerg Med	1.50	1.44	1.27	1.11	1.11	1.90	0.96	0.86	1.48	1.85	0.63	0.90	0.61
Obstet Gyn	1.16	0.81	1.33	2.53	1.68	2.19	0.94	1.10	1.97	1.59	0.83	1.20	1.92
Surg Genl	0.97	1.06	0.85	0.76	2.20	1.57	0.61	0.50	1.36	1.22	0.47	0.61	0.40
Surg Spec	0.95	1.14	0.98	0.70	2.19	1.65	0.60	0.54	1.32	1.08	0.52	0.82	0.41
Occup Med	1.65	1.35	1.57	1.23	1.23	1.95	1.34	0.83	1.98	1.97	0.92	1.22	0.74
Other	1.16	1.07	1.31	1.10	1.48	1.89	0.95	0.71	1.44	1.50	0.72	1.07	0.58
R-Square	0.23	0.14	0.25	0.34	0.18	0.14	0.12	0.28	0.23	0.38	0.10	0.11	0.18

Response Categories:

3.00 > 2.51 = I plan, support, and counsel.
2.50 > 2.00 > 1.51 = I recommend specific courses of action.
1.50 > 1.00 > 0.51 = I give general information.
0.50 > 0.00 = Someone else in practice is responsible.

Source: 1985 Role Delineation Study, American Academy of Physician Assistants, internal documentation.

CONCLUSION

Health promotion and disease prevention are an important part of public health and will contribute to the health of the nation in measurable ways in the coming years. However, individual responsibilities for maintaining healthy lifestyles must be complemented by a society that embraces values that support a clean and safe environment and uses its resources for the benefit of the public at large. As we have seen, those values must also incorporate a plan for care of all of the citizens, for the public health of the nation depends on providing a basic level of food, shelter, and safety to all.

NOTES

1. Susan S. Addiss, "Setting Goals and Priorities," *American Journal of Public Health* 75 (1985):1276–1280.
2. Alfred Yankauer, *"The American Journal of Public Health, 1911–1985,"* *American Journal of Public Health* 76 (1986):809–815.
3. Ibid., p. 810.
4. Dan Beauchamp, "Public Health as Social Justice," in *Public Health and the Law: Issues and Trends,* ed. L. Hogie (Rockville, MD: Aspen Publishers, 1980), p. 6.
5. Anthony Robbins, "Public Health in the Next Decade," *Journal of Public Health Policy,* December 1985, pp. 440–446.
6. Michael R. Pollard, Gary S. Persinger, and Joseph G. Perpich, "Technology Innovation in Health Care," *Health Affairs,* Summer, 1986, pp. 135–147.
7. Louis Garrison and Gail Wilensky, "Cost Containment and Incentives for Technology," *Health Affairs,* Summer, 1986, p. 47.
8. Henry J. Aaron, "Questioning the Cost of Biomedical Research," *Health Affairs,* Summer, 1986, pp. 96–99.
9. Jeffrey M. Prottas, "The Structure and Effectiveness of the U.S. Organ Procurement System," *Inquiry* 22 (1985):366.
10. Ibid., p. 366.
11. Mary Ann Bailey, "'Rationing' and American Health Policy," *Journal of Health Politics, Policy and Law* 9 (1984):489–501.
12. Henry Aaron, *The Painful Prescription* (Washington, DC: Brookings Institution, 1984), p. 34.
13. James W. Curran and W. Meade Morgan, "Acquired Immune Deficiency Syndrome," in *AIDS from the Beginning,* ed. Helene Cole and George Lundberg (Chicago: American Medical Association, 1986), p. XXI.
14. Institute of Medicine, *Mobilizing Against AIDS* (Cambridge, MA: Harvard University Press, 1987), p. 15.
15. D.P. Francis and V. Chin, "The Prevention of Acquired Immunodeficiency Syndrome in the United States," *Journal of the American Medical Association* 257 (1987):1357–1366.
16. P. Black, "HTLV-III, AIDS, and the Brain," *New England Journal of Medicine* 313 (1985):1538–1539.

17. L.B. Moskowitz, G.T. Hensley, and J.C. Chan. "The Neuropathy of Acquired Immunodeficiency Syndrome," *Archives of Pathology and Laboratory Medicine* 108 (1984):867–872.

18. *Coping with AIDS*. 1986. US Dept of Health and Human Services, p. 15.

19. Ronald Bayer, "The AIDS Crisis," *Journal of Health Politics, Policy and Law* 11 (1986):172.

20. JoAnne Bennett, "What We Know About AIDS," *American Journal of Nursing* 86 (1986):1016–1020.

21. Victor Sidel, "War or Peace: Smallpox and the Use and Abuse of Public Health," *American Journal of Public Health* 76 (1986):1189–1190.

22. Arnold Relman, "The Physician's Role in Preventing Nuclear War," *New England Journal of Medicine* 315 (1986):889–890.

23. *Highlights from the National Survey on Drug Abuse*. 1983. US Dept of Health and Human Services, p. 1.

24. William McAuliffe, et al., "Psychoactive Drug Use Among Practicing Physicians and Medical Students," *New England Journal of Medicine* 315 (1986):805–809.

25. A.S. Golden, D.E. Carlson, and J.L. Hagan, *The Art of Teaching Primary Care* (New York: Springer Publishing Co., 1981).

Chapter 6

The Physician Assistant in Hospitals

Carol James is a physician assistant working in neurosurgery at the Johns Hopkins Hospital in Baltimore. She is a graduate of the Yale University Physician Assistant Program and chairs the Professional Practices and Relations Committee of the Maryland Academy of Physician Assistants.

James Cawley: Describe the duties of your position.

Carol James: I spend about three-quarters of my time assisting the Chief of pediatric neurosurgery on surgical cases. I am usually first or second assistant in the operating room and assist in the pre- and postoperative care of these patients. I also coordinate the pediatric neuro-oncology clinic where outpatients are followed. I'm also closely involved, along with my other supervising physician, in the adult chronic pain clinic.

James Cawley: What is your role in this clinic?

Carol James: One of my supervisors, Dr. North, and I run a clinic where we see patients with chronic pain secondary to previous spinal cord surgery, arachnoiditis, and other intractable pain problems. We implant externally programmable epidural electrical stimulators to alleviate chronic pain in these patients. I do the complete inservice education program for the patient, first assist at the implantation of the permanent system, do all of the perioperative programming of the stimulator, and instruct the patient after implantation on how to use the device. We have had very good results.

James Cawley: What is your interaction with the residents on your service?

Carol James: We have a very large residency program in Neurosurgery here at Hopkins. I provide the continuity of care for the service, particularly in the clinic because the residents change so frequently. Also, none of the residents has experience with the epidural stimulator, only myself and my supervisor.

James Cawley: What is your relationship with your supervisor?

Carol James: We're very good friends. He just asked me to be the god-mother to one of his children. We obviously work very closely together not only in the operating room but also in the clinics we run. It's very much a team approach.

James Cawley: How does the hospital recognize your position?

Carol James: All of the physician assistants at Johns Hopkins are classi-fied as Affiliate Members of the medical staff. The Credentials Committee of the medical staff reviews the qualifications and credentials of the physi-cian assistants and approves our scope of function.

James Cawley: Do you feel that your salary is commensurate with your responsibilities?

Carol James: It is much better than in the past. Several years ago, the Human Resources Department wanted to make physician assistants salaried employees of the hospital with pay levels commensurate with nursing salary scales. This proposal did not work for many of us because it did not take into consideration our level of responsibility and the fact that most physician assistants here work more than a 40-hour week. We now are paid a reasonable hourly rate based on the amount of hours worked. This is better, but I'm still not sure I'm paid what I feel I'm worth. Dr. Carson and I are discussing this with the Human Resources Department.

James Cawley: What attracted you to a hospital-based position?

Carol James: I was familiar with the hospital environment prior to becoming a physician assistant. I'm very oriented to the team approach that is part of hospital medicine. I like being in an academically oriented setting as well. Strange as it may sound, being in the hospital affords me an oppor-tunity not only to become involved in advanced levels of patient care but also allows me to do patient counseling and education. If I were in private practice, I doubt that I would have the time to do this. For each patient that I see as a candidate for the stimulator, I do 6 to 8 hours worth of direct patient education in preparation for the implantation of the epidural stimulator.

James Cawley: In your view, what are the important issues facing hospital-based physician assistants?

Carol James: I'm not sure that most administrators know or understand the role of the physician assistant in the hospital. Many of them feel that physician assistants are some type of glorified technician. They do not realize the educational preparation and credentialing processes that physi-cian assistants go through. Things are improving. Within specific depart-ments, the physician assistants are well respected, but overall there is still much education to be done.

THE PHYSICIAN ASSISTANT IN HOSPITALS

The hospital is the setting for the delivery of most acute medical care. Because one of the major objectives of this book is to describe the extent of physician assistant utilization in the health care system, it is important to explore the roles that physician assistants fulfill in the hospital setting and to examine various aspects relevant to their employment, impact, and contributions in these institutions.

EXTENT OF UTILIZATION

Hospital settings are the fastest growing area of physician assistant employment. About 14 percent of the total physician assistant population were employed by hospitals in 1976; one decade later, about 33 percent were working in hospitals. If one accepts as accurate the estimate of the total physician assistant population in 1987 as approximately 18,000, fully 6,000 physician assistants are employed in the hospital setting.[1] Recent employment trends indicate that these numbers are likely to increase steadily.[2]

Physician assistants are employed in a wide variety of hospitals, ranging from small community hospitals to large academic medical centers. A significant number of medium to large community hospitals employ physician assistants, as do many hospitals who utilize them in affiliated units, such as outpatient clinics, employee health clinics, and emergency departments.[3-6] Also, several large hospital networks that provide medical care services to prison populations[7] and elderly populations[8] employ physician assistants. Many physician assistants who work in private solo or group practices also spend portions of their time caring for the practice's hospitalized patients.

Physician assistants began to be utilized by hospitals shortly after the concept of the new profession was developed in the late 1960s. The first hospital to use physician assistants was Duke University Medical Center, the site of the first physician assistant program. Soon thereafter, Montefiore Hospital in New York began using physician assistants. (For a more detailed description of this event, see Chapter 9.) At about the same time, other large university teaching centers who also sponsored physician assistant educational programs began to hire their graduates for the inpatient setting. Such teaching hospitals include the Yale-New Haven Medical Center (Connecticut), the Marshfield Clinic (Wisconsin),[9] Alderson-Broaddus Hospital (West Virginia), Geisinger Medical Center (Danville, Pennsylvania), Hahnemann Hospital (Philadelphia, Pennsylvania), University of Nebraska Medical Center (Omaha), Baylor University Medical Center (Houston, Texas), and the George Washington University Medical Center (Washington, DC), among others.[10] Many other large hospitals that were not directly involved in physician assistant training also hired physician assistants for inpatient care roles.

These included Beth Israel Hospital in New York,[11] Baltimore City Hospital, the Johns Hopkins Hospital, Genesee Hospital in Rochester, the Cleveland Clinic, Maine Medical Center, Mary Imogene Bassett Hospital in Cooperstown, New York, and Long Island Jewish-Queens Hospital Center in New York City. The patterns of experiences with physician assistants in these institutions have been replicated in numerous medium to small nonteaching hospitals.

Physician assistants are also utilized extensively in Veterans Administration hospitals, the largest hospital system in the country. Physician assistants began working in the VA system early in the history of the profession (1968), and their employment is well established there. As of 1986, at least 500 physician assistants were employed by the VA system, with most of them working in inpatient roles on medical and surgical wards.[12]

As the concept of utilizing physician assistants in the inpatient setting spread and gained wider acceptance, other noted institutions began in the late 1970s to hire them. At present, prominent hospitals such as Brigham and Women's in Boston, Columbia-Presbyterian in New York, Grady Memorial in Atlanta, LA County-USC Medical Center in Los Angeles, Cook County in Chicago, and the Detroit Medical Center employ physician assistants in various capacities.

Several changes in health manpower utilization over the past 10 years have led to the increasing employment of physician assistants as inpatient providers. These include:

- a decrease in the size and number of physician residency programs in major fields (surgery, medicine, pediatrics) and changes in the accreditation policies of these programs
- a decrease in the number of foreign medical graduates (FMGs) entering U.S. graduate medical education programs
- changing federal rules and regulations governing reimbursement of hospitals.[13]

In combination, these changes led hospitals to restructure the staffing patterns of inpatient wards so that, on the one hand, patient care services and quality of care could be maintained, and on the other, the provision of resident teaching experiences and the production of fully trained physician specialists could be more appropriately balanced.

Once it became clear that physician assistants could fulfill inpatient roles traditionally held by interns and residents,[14] hospitals became very interested in developing alternate staffing arrangements in which physician assistants worked in conjunction with senior residents and attending physicians. Surgery was one of the first fields in which physician assistants were employed in large numbers. In a survey conducted by Perry in 1979, it was found that over one-third of departments of surgery in large teaching institutions (over 400 beds) employed physician assistants.[14] By the early 1980s, the trend of the utilization of physician assistants as housestaff had become well established, had spread quickly to hospitals of all varieties, and had expanded the types of roles and employment opportunities available to newly graduating physician assistants.

INPATIENT ROLES AND FUNCTIONS

The initial thrust of physician assistant education was the training of primary care practitioners. It was not anticipated in the early days of the development of the profession that large numbers of physician assistants would be utilized in the inpatient sector. Nonetheless, when hospitals began to hire physician assistants it became quickly apparent that these providers could assume those tasks and functions required in the inpatient setting.[15]

One of the most basic and important skills taught to all physician assistant students is the performance of a medical history and physical examination. These are the "bread and butter" skills of physician assistants, and their application is relevant to virtually all medical settings. Most hospitals require that a complete history and physical be done on all newly admitted patients. Typically, these tasks are performed by physician medical housestaff, usually interns and junior residents. When physician assistants began to assume inpatient roles, they often were used in roles similar to those of interns or junior residents. The function of performing the admission history and physical was a task that physician assistants were well suited to fulfill.[16]

Yet, the inpatient duties assumed by physician assistants quickly went far beyond the performance of the admission history and physical examination. As the utilization of physician assistants as hospital housestaff became more widespread, their duties expanded to include a full range of responsibilities that in the past had been the sole domain of physicians.[17]

Housestaff Roles

The majority of physician assistants employed in the hospital setting work in roles that are frequently termed as "physician assistant housestaff."[17] In a broad sense, these roles comprise duties that commonly fall to the intern or junior resident. A typical job description of a housestaff physician assistant is presented in Exhibit 6-1.

In addition to "physician assistant housestaff," other terms used to describe hospital physician assistants are "staff associates," "staff assistants," "inpatient physician assistants," or, according to Silver and McAtee, "associate resi-

Exhibit 6-1 Typical Job Description of a Housestaff Physician Assistant

---

The physician assistant, as a member of the ancillary health care team, will function to provide medical/surgical support to the attending physicians, nurses, and patients, and may perform the following functions:

1. Review patient records to aid in determining health status
2. Take patient histories, perform physical examinations, and identify normal and abnormal findings on histories, physicals, and commonly performed laboratory studies. Information collected is to be presented to the supervising physician.
3. Perform developmental screening exams on children
4. Record pertinent patient data in the medical record
5. Carry out or relay a physician's orders for diagnostic procedures, treatments, and medication in accordance with existing drug laws. The assistant may transcribe the orders in the patient chart as a verbal or telephone order from the physician and signed by the assistant. All orders written by physician assistants will be countersigned by the physician within 24 hours of initiation of the order.
6. Collect specimens for commonly performed blood counts: urine, sputum, stool analysis, and cultures
7. Perform the following clinical procedures subject to individual credentialing:
   A. Venipuncture/arteriopuncture
   B. Electrocardiogram recording
   C. Administer intravenous medications and contrast materials for radiologic studies; collect fluids, blood, and blood components upon order from an attending/supervising physician
   D. Administer injections: intramuscular, intravenous, or intradermal
   E. Administer intradermal skin tests
   F. Nasogastric intubation
   G. Endotracheal intubation
   H. Insertion of urinary catheters
   I. Cleansing and debridement of wounds
   J. Administer local infiltrative anesthesia
   K. Suture lacerations: Injuries involving arteries, tendons, or nerves must be examined by the supervising physician prior to the institution of therapy
   L. Application of dressings, bandages, and splints
   M. Application and removal of orthopedic casts
   N. Cardiopulmonary resuscitation
8. Assist in surgery, fulfilling all requirements of a surgical assistant
9. Do pre- and postoperative surgical/medical care
10. Provide patient education
11. Be available for "Call" as determined by the department
12. Screen patients to determine need for medical attention

In the event of any change in the patient's condition, the assistant will:

1. Obtain a history and do a physical exam appropriate to the change
2. After the initial patient assessment, if it is necessary to complete the evaluation, the physician assistant may initiate the following laboratory tests:
   A. Complete blood count
   B. Differential, platelets

Exhibit 6-1 continued

    C. Prothrombin time
    D. Partial thromboplastin time
    E. Electrolytes
    F. Blood urea nitrogen
    G. Glucose
    H. Amylase
    I. Arterial blood gas
    J. Urinalysis
    K. Gram stain of secretions
    L. Chest x-ray
    M. Abdominal x-ray—flatplate, upright, and/or decubitus
    N. Electrocardiogram
    O. X-ray of extremities

dents.''[18] Regardless of the particular label applied to them, these physician assistants are functioning as integral parts of the inpatient residency team. As Silver states, ''as permanent members of the housestaff and salaried employees of the hospital, they provide continuity on a hospital service over a much longer period of time than can first-year physician residents.''[18]

The clinical responsibilities assumed by physician assistants in inpatient roles are extensive. The services in which physician assistants are most commonly employed are inpatient medical, surgical, and pediatric wards. Some institutions use physician assistant housestaff on psychiatric and OB/GYN services.

The duties and privileges of physician assistants vary somewhat from hospital to hospital, depending upon such factors as how many physician assistants are employed on the service, the extent of resident and attending physician coverage and supervision, the credentialing policies of the institution, the latitude allowed to the hospital and the physician assistant by the state medical practice laws, and reimbursement policies.

Not infrequently, the clinical roles of housestaff physician assistants go beyond the standard typical list of functions described in Exhibit 6-1. For example, if the housestaff physician assistant works on an internal or general medical floor, the physician assistant, by virtue of his or her experience and on-the-job training, and with the approval of the credentials committee of the hospital, may assume such additional duties as the performance of certain procedures—bone marrow aspiration, thoracentesis, paracentesis, or lumbar puncture. Also, housestaff physician assistants may be involved in clinical research activities, collecting specialized data on patients, monitoring experimental drug and therapeutic efforts, and following established research protocols. If the hospital is a teaching institution, the housestaff physician assistant often participates in teaching rounds, may assist in the training of third-year medical students and/or second-year physician assistant students, and be involved in other clinical educational activities.[17]

The role of the physician assistant as inpatient housestaff has become fairly well established in many hospitals. Commonly, institutions employ from 6 to 12 physician assistants covering, with residents and attending physicians, services of 50 to 150 beds. Sometimes physician assistant housestaff duties encompass periods of emergency room or outpatient clinic duties, depending on service and institutional needs.

Continuity of care is perceived as a key advantage of the utilization of physician assistants as inpatient providers. Another advantage for those hospitals that maintain physician residency programs is that using physician assistants allows chiefs of service to reduce the numbers of physician residents to be trained, thus balancing service (patient care) needs with educational requirements.

There is a large body of evidence that attests to the high quality of care delivered by physician assistants in ambulatory patient care settings.[19] Although no studies have looked specifically at physician assistants in the inpatient setting, the empirical evidence observed by many hospitals using them as housestaff suggests that quality of care is maintained at high levels. Silver states that physician assistants working in these roles "function with a degree of skill and competence similar to that of first-year physician residents in the same position."[18]

Specialty Inpatient Roles

Hospital-based physician assistants are also working in roles that are specialty oriented. Often, after 1 or 2 years of general housestaff experience they assume more specialized roles in hospital settings (see Chapter 9 for a more extended discussion of physician assistant specialization). For example, physician assistants are employed in surgical subspecialties, such as cardiothoracic surgery, neurosurgery, orthopedic surgery, or urologic surgery, where their duties not only involve some or many of the tasks of the typical housestaff physician assistant but also include specialty-oriented clinical duties and procedures. For example, the physician assistant who works in orthopedics may do regular housestaff functions on the orthopedic service, assist at surgery in orthopedic procedures, participate in orthopedic rounds, perform routine specialized procedures and diagnostic testing, and develop particular competence in orthopedic evaluation and management.

Physician assistant roles in cardiothoracic surgery services have expanded at particularly rapid rates, and it is estimated that there are anywhere from 500 to 750 physician assistants working in this field alone, usually in academic medical centers or teaching institutions. They perform a wide range of duties on these services, including preoperative evaluation and preparation of the patient, intra-operative assisting (harvesting the saphenous vein, establishing cardiopulmonary bypass, and controlling bleeding and closure of the incision), postoperative management of the patient in both the intensive care unit and later on the wards, and a variety of other clinical, teaching, and administrative functions.[20] A number of physician assistants work in anesthesiology as well.

Physician assistants are also working in a number of the internal medicine sub-specialties—cardiology, pulmonology, gastroenterology, renal medicine, rheumatology, infectious disease, and oncology. In these disciplines, they not only participate in routine patient care duties but also perform specialty-oriented technical procedures. Physician assistants who work in cardiology, for example, perform or assist in performing exercise stress tests, coronary angiography, and similar invasive diagnostic tests. Those who work in oncology develop particular skills in bone marrow aspiration, thoracentesis and paracentesis, and the administration of intravenous chemotherapy. Physician assistants employed on a pulmonary medicine service become proficient in various pulmonary function tests and the utilization of respirators.

Some other specialties in which physician assistants work include neurology, ENT, ophthalmology, the intensive care and burn units, dermatology, urology and urodynamics, renal dialysis, geriatrics, radiology, neonatology, pathology, allergy and immunology, and emergency medicine. In these disciplines, physician assistants work closely with the physician specialists, nurses, technicians, and other health professions on the specialty team. Although they develop high levels of competency in these areas, their duties are specific to the particular service or institution in which they work. In some cases, the skills of these physician assistants have been transferable, but not enough experience has been obtained as yet with these groups to establish definite career mobility patterns.

Additional formal training is now available for specialty areas. A master's degree training program in critical care medicine is available to graduate physician assistants at the Emory University Medical Center. Presently three university centers provide formal 1-year specialty training programs for physician assistants in pediatrics or neonatology. (See Table 9-1 in Chapter 9.)

In an effort to describe more fully the physician assistants' inpatient specialty roles, McKelvey and colleagues from the University of Iowa conducted a survey of 23 physician assistants employed by that institution.[21] Using both a written questionnaire and personal interview, they found that four physician assistants were in general medicine, one in general surgery, and the remainder were in various subspecialties, i.e., four in cardiothoracic surgery, two in pediatric cardiology and urologic oncology, three in hematology, and one each in radiology, psychiatry, occupational health, gynecologic oncology, urology, burn care, and cardiology. The self-reported role activities of these providers and the mean percentage time spent in each activity comprised five areas: technical/procedural (18 percent), patient care (59.1 percent), administration (10.7 percent), research (5.2 percent), and medical education (6.2 percent). Patient education was identified as an important component of physician assistant patient care activities, taking from 25 percent of all patient care time in surgical specialties to 55 percent of patient care time in pediatrics. Of interest, when physician assistant estimates of their activities were compared to physician supervisor estimates, over 75 percent of the physicians significantly underestimated the extent of physician assistant activity in patient education.

Mixed Clinical/Nonclinical Roles

In addition to serving as physician assistant housestaff and in specialty inpatient roles in the hospital setting, some physician assistants fulfill a third role that can be termed a mixed clinical/nonclinical role. Although all inpatient physician assistants perform some nonclinical duties, this role category includes those positions in which nonclinical duties take up the majority of the individual's time.

One such role is the chief physician assistant on a housestaff service. Referred to variously as the physician assistant "manager," the physician assistant "administrator," or some such similar designation, the chief physician assistant serves in a primarily administrative capacity over all the physician assistants working in an institution. They serve in a supervisory role; manage the assignments and schedules of housestaff physician assistants; develop protocols, rules, and procedures governing physician assistant employment in the hospital; coordinate teaching and patient care activities involving physician assistants; and represent the physician assistant staff to the medical and administrative hierarchy of the institution. The chief physician assistant may have clinical responsibilities as well.

It is not uncommon for large hospitals to employ as many as 60 to 80 physician assistants located in a wide variety of departments. Although some work directly for individual physicians in subspecialty departments, the general housestaff physician assistants usually are designated administratively as members of medical or surgical departments. Within these departments, physician chiefs may appoint a physician assistant to administer the staff of the 15 to 25 physician assistants who work on the service. Although these chief physician assistants do not supervise the clinical activities of the staff physician assistants, they are responsible for the aforementioned administrative matters involving the physician assistant staff.

Another primarily nonclinical role assumed by some physician assistants in hospitals involves medical research. A number of physician assistants combine bench laboratory duties, clinical responsibilities, management of the research data base, participation in the analysis of experimental results, and the generation of scientific communication.[22] In the past physician assistants have been involved in clinical research projects involving areas such as infections in immunocompromised patients, sexually transmitted diseases, prehospital management of heart attack victims, trials of chemotherapeutic agents, and pancreatic islet cell transplant programs. Physician assistants also work in community screening programs for cancer patients, in epidemiologic and clinical investigations of AIDS, and in geriatric screening programs. Some are also active in health services research projects studying HMO staffing effectiveness and other aspects of health manpower usage.

Yet another group of physician assistants have moved into hospital-based administrative roles. They are employed, for example, as managers of hospital-affiliated ambulatory clinics or assistant directors of medical education. Physician assistants are also involved in preadmission certification programs, utilization review, quality assurance, DRG coordination, and medical information systems programs. The involvement of physician assistants in these types of areas seems to be broadening and to be limited only by the interest and ambition of the physician assistants involved. In some instances, entry into administrative roles has been facilitated by the physician assistant obtaining formal graduate education in a discipline relevant to the job. For example, a physician assistant who seeks a job in medical information systems management may need, in addition to physician assistant training, a master's degree in computer science.

It is likely that in the future more physician assistants will move into such hospital-based administrative areas. The profession as a whole is only little more than 20 years old, and the mean age of all physician assistants is only 34 years. Many physician assistants who hold full-time clinical positions are pursuing various types of graduate degrees in business, health administration, public health, or law that will allow them to compete for high-level administrative positions in hospital systems. That they also hold a respected clinical credential with patient care experience can only assist them in achieving this type of professional advancement.

PRIVILEGES, SUPERVISION, AND CREDENTIALING

Webster's Dictionary defines supervision as "the act of direction or management." The adequate supervision of a physician assistant has been a topic of both controversy and concern since the inception of the profession. Supervision may be either direct or indirect. When a physician does direct or "over the shoulder" supervision of a physician assistant, the purpose of employing an assistant is defeated. The need to provide this type of supervision, especially in a hospital, renders the physician assistant basically useless. Doing so is time consuming for the physician, frustrating to the physician assistant, and damaging to the relationship between the physician and the physician assistant.

Even though the physician assistant is a dependent practitioner, he or she must develop and exercise some degree of independent clinical judgment. The parameters for the application of physician assistant clinical judgment are usually defined, first of all, by the existing medical practice statutes of the state governing physician assistants and their scope of practice. In addition to state regulations, each hospital must develop specific institutional guidelines governing the activities of employed physician assistants. The process through which these guidelines are developed and applied is termed *credentialing*.

Traditionally, hospitals review and approve the qualifications and backgrounds of physicians before granting them specific privileges, i.e., admitting patients, performing surgery, etc. Commonly, a credentials committee comprised of physicians who hold privileges at a hospital will establish rules and guidelines whereby a provider can apply to the hospital seeking certain privileges. The committee then reviews the qualifications of that provider and grants specific privileges or takes other appropriate action. The provider is then authorized to perform the delineated duties within that institution.

The process by which most hospitals govern physician assistants is patterned after this type of credentialing system. Typically, guidelines delineating the duties of a physician assistant are developed by the credentials committee of the medical staff of the institution. These guidelines take into consideration the expected clinical duties that they will perform, the specific needs and requirements of the medical attending staff, the expected training and qualifications of the physician assistant, and provisions regarding supervision and monitoring of their performance. An important part of these guidelines is a specific physician assistant job description. Commonly, job descriptions must be developed for each type of service on which they work, i.e., medicine, surgery, pediatrics, etc. Although certain common functions are applicable to all services, specific duties on each will vary. The job description must be specific enough to accommodate these variations.

The credentialing guidelines specify what types of educational and professional qualifications the physician assistant must have to receive privileges. Typically a physician assistant candidate will be required to be (1) a graduate of a CAHEA (Council on Allied Health Education and Accreditation) approved physician assistant training program, (2) eligible for or to have passed the national certifying examination administered by the NCCPA (National Commission on Certification of Physician Assistants), and (3) registered properly with the state board of medical examiners. In addition to these basic qualifications, credentials committees may prefer that a physician assistant have prior inpatient clinical experience or formal clinical training in a specific area.

Once reviewed and approved by the credentialing committee, the physician assistant is granted limited medical staff privileges. In this context, the physician assistant may be designated as ''staff affiliate,'' ''associate staff,'' or a similar title indicating that he or she is a member of that institution's medical staff.

Typically, a number of stipulations accompany the granting of medical staff privileges to inpatient physician assistants. These often specify tasks or actions that a physician assistant may not perform, such as prescribing certain types of medications or admitting patients, discharging patients, etc., in the absence of physician supervision. Stipulations also concern the writing of orders on the patient's chart, usually with specific provision made for physician countersignature.

In some institutions, the credentialing process mandates a temporary orientation period prior to the granting of full privileges. During this orientation period, the physician assistant performs certain basic tasks outlined in the job description, but not every one. For example, during this period, the physician assistant may only be permitted to perform admission histories and physical examinations and order routine tests, but not to write orders. During this orientation period, the performance of the physician assistant is monitored by supervising physicians and/or the chief physician assistant. After this 60- to 90-day period, he or she may then be granted full physician assistant staff privileges in accordance with the credentials committee guidelines. In some hospitals, the final approval mechanisms involve the Board of Trustees as well. In some institutions, the credentialing process may also include the opportunity for physician assistants to obtain "extended" privileges—ones that go beyond the basic job description. For example, once a physician assistant obtains basic privileges, he or she then may go on to demonstrate proficiency and apply for privileges to perform specialty roles, such as insertion of arterial catheters or advanced cardiac life support. These advanced privileges are then included in the physician assistant's permanent medical staff files.

The process by which physician assistants can be granted limited staff privileges in hospital settings is now fairly standard. However, the course by which this process was developed was not always a smooth one. Initially, in many hospitals, there were a wide variety of barriers that prevented physician assistants from obtaining hospital privileges. Such barriers included the medical staff members' unfamiliarity with the physician assistant concept, concerns about the legal status of physician assistants, malpractice and liability issues, opposition from the hospital nursing staff, and legal questions regarding the writing of orders by nonphysicians. Although education by physician assistants regarding their roles and experience with physician assistants in the performance of their duties have in many instances allayed these concerns, these issues continue to be problematic in some circumstances.

A special situation involving hospital privileges for physician assistants concerns the private practitioner who hires a physician assistant and seeks to obtain hospital privileges for him or her. If the hospital already employs full-time house-staff physician assistants and has an established process of physician assistant credentialing, there usually is little difficulty in awarding privileges. If the hospital, however, has had no experience with physician assistants, a sometimes long and difficult process must be instituted. Often, to develop guidelines and/or job descriptions for the granting of limited medical staff privileges, the hospital's bylaws must be amended. In a hospital that has made an administrative decision to employ physician assistant housestaff, this revision process may not be too difficult. Yet, in an institution unfamiliar with physician assistants that is faced with the question of credentialing only one or two physician assistants employed by a private practitioner, the task may be formidable.[23]

A number of state hospital associations, state medical societies, and institutions employing physician assistants themselves have published guidelines to assist hospitals in developing bylaws provisions and other written policies. One such document, *Hospital Guidelines for Utilizing Physician Assistants,* published by the Maryland Hospital Association provides a series of recommendations regarding the definition of who can qualify for hospital privileges, procedures for appointment, adoption of job descriptions, supervision, prohibitions, and general functions.[24] In Pennsylvania, the state medical society distributed a paper by Nathan Hershey entitled ''A Guide for Developing Bylaw Provisions in Hospitals for Credentialing Limited Health Practitioners.'' Guidelines and documents from the Geisinger Medical Center in Pennsylvania, a large tertiary care institution well known for its experience in employing physician assistants, have been distributed and utilized by many institutions seeking advice on how best to establish effective and uniform physician assistant policies.[25] In addition, the AAPA has developed model guidelines for amending hospital medical staff bylaws (Exhibit 6-2).

The American Hospital Association has also published several documents outlining bylaw policy recommendations; on the whole, these are quite supportive of the utilization of physician assistants.[26] The AHA recommends that physician assistants be integrated into the medical staff as ''staff affiliates'' and governed by a single set of bylaws. This process should be accomplished through the hospital's credentials committee or other appropriate committee of the medical staff. The credentials committee should be responsible for reviewing the application of the individual physician assistant and making recommendations to the hospital's governing board regarding the extent of clinical function and the specific privileges to be awarded.[27]

Although it does not have a specific policy pertaining to the use of physician assistants, the Joint Commission on Accreditation of Hospitals (JCAH) supports the concept that physician assistants can ''exercise judgment within their areas of competency and participate directly in the management of patients under physician supervision.''[28] The accreditation standards of the JCAH allow hospitals to utilize physician assistants as members of the medical staff and provide details regarding bylaws amendments that permit the credentialing and utilization of physician assistants. Considering that the entire issue of hospital privileges for various types of nonphysician providers (podiatrists, physician assistants, nurse

Exhibit 6-2 Guidelines for Amending Hospital Staff Bylaws

In order to provide patient care services in the hospital, physician assistants and their supervising physicians must seek delineation of their clinical privileges. The process of delineating clinical privileges includes three elements: establishing criteria for privileges, evaluating an applicant's qualifications, and matching the individual practitioner's skills to the needs and resources of the hospital. The criteria and process for granting clinical privileges to physician assistants should be outlined in the medical staff bylaws. The following guidelines are intended to assist physicians and physician assistants in seeking amendments to hospital medical staff bylaws that would authorize the granting of clinical privileges to physician assistants.

These guidelines do not contain model bylaw amendment language that can be directly incorporated into existing medical staff bylaws. Rather, they are intended to be a general guide that can be applied and adapted to suit the unique requirements of each hospital. This document enumerates the important elements that should be considered and provides a brief discussion of each element. It is suggested that a medical staff considering amendments to its bylaws consult with legal counsel.

Definition of Physician Assistant

Medical staff bylaws generally begin with a preamble that includes definitions of important terms that are frequently used in the bylaws. A definition of physician assistant should be included in the preamble. This definition should generally conform to the definition used in state law and should approximate the generic definition of a physician assistant used by the AAPA. The following definition serves as an example.

A *physician assistant* (PA) is a person qualified by academic and clinical training to provide patient services under the supervision of a qualified physician member of the medical staff who maintains overall responsibility for the performance of that assistant.

Composition of the Medical Staff

Membership on the medical staff enables practitioners to diagnose illness and perform other functions in the hospital. Additionally, medical staff membership provides practitioners with a voice in developing and implementing hospital and medical staff policies. However, admission to the medical staff does not carry with it automatic clinical privileges, and failure to obtain membership on the medical staff does not necessarily prevent a qualified practitioner from practicing in the hospital.

Medical staff bylaws identify the categories of practitioners eligible for medical staff membership. Consideration should be given to including physician assistants among the categories of practitioners eligible for membership on the medical staff. An alternative type of medical staff membership, other than the full membership reserved for physicians, might be considered.

Requirements for Membership on the Medical Staff

Medical staff bylaws should specify uniform criteria for granting initial and continuing membership on the medical staff. As applies to physician assistants these criteria might include evidence of current state registration, relevant training and/or experience, certification, current competence, physical and mental health status, and evidence of adequate professional liability insurance.

Exhibit 6-2 continued

Clinical Privileges

The medical staff bylaws should stipulate that all clinical privileges granted to physician assistants be consistent with all applicable state laws and regulations and that a physician assistant may only render patient care services that are within the scope of practice of the supervising physician.

The criteria for delineating the clinical privileges of physician assistants should be specified in the bylaws. Criteria for granting clinical privileges might include evidence of current state registration, relevant training and experience, current competence, and present health status. Additional criteria might include evidence of adequate liability insurance and information on any past or pending professional liability and disciplinary actions.

The process for granting clinical privileges is usually discussed in four places in the bylaws: the article concerned with clinical privileges, the article describing the structure of the credentials committee, the article describing the duties of department chairmen, and the article describing hearing procedures. The process of granting clinical privileges may vary considerably from one hospital to another, but generally the process should (1) be completed in a timely fashion; (2) if they exist, department chairmen should make specific recommendations for clinical privileges; (3) an appeal mechanism for adverse decisions should exist; and (4) the governing board should have ultimate authority to grant clinical privileges. An application for renewal of clinical privileges should be processed in essentially the same manner as that for granting initial privileges.

In regard to physician assistants the medical staff or a unit of the medical staff should bear responsibility for reviewing initial and renewal applications for clinical privileges and for making a recommendation to the governing board.

There are at least four basic methods of delineating clinical privileges: a list of procedures; categorization according to severity of illness, level of training, or degree of required supervision; self-description; or a combination of approaches. Regardless of the method of delineating clinical privileges used, specific privileges for physician assistants either as individual practitioners or as a group should not be spelled out in the bylaws.

Corrective Action

The criteria and process for disciplining physician assistants should be spelled out in the bylaws. The process should generally conform to the process applied to physician members of the medical staff.

Due Process

The bylaws should give the physician assistant the right to request the initiation of due process procedures when actions taken by the medical staff or the governing board adversely affect his or her clinical privileges. Due process procedures for physician assistants should generally parallel those available to physician members of the medical staff.

Quality Assurance

The bylaws should provide for effective mechanisms to carry out quality assurance responsibilities with respect to physician assistants. These mechanisms should include regular monitoring and evaluation by the supervising physician.